THE COMPLETE GUIDE TO THE BELGIAN MALINOIS

Tarah Schwartz

Publication Data

Tarah Schwartz

The Complete Guide to the Belgian Malinois_First edition.

Summary: "Successfully raising a Belgian Malinois from puppy to old age" — Provided by publisher.

ISBN: 978-1-952069-80-2

[1.Belgian Malinois — Non-Fiction] I. Title.

This book has been written with the published intent to provide accurate and authoritative information in regard to the subject matter included. While every reasonable precaution has been taken in preparation of this book the author and publisher expressly disclaim responsibility for any errors, omissions, or adverse effects arising from the use or application of the information contained inside. The techniques and suggestions are to be used at the reader's discretion and are not to be considered a substitute for professional veterinary care. If you suspect a medical problem with your dog, consult your veterinarian.
Design by Sorin Rădulescu
First paperback edition, 2020

TABLE OF CONTENTS

APTER 13

e Belgian Malinois in Work and Sport **113**

APTER 14

trition **129**

APTER 15

ysical and Mental Exercise **143**

CHAPTER 1
The History of the Belgian Malinois

The Origins of the Belgian Malinois

"The Belgian Malinois 'breed' is only a designated breed in the United States. All other countries Malinois is a type in the Belgian Shepherd breed."

JANET WOLFF
Stahlrosenhof Intl K-9

Photo Courtesy of
Janine Blanks

As the name suggests, the Belgian Malinois was originally developed in Belgium in the late 1800s as one of four varieties of Belgian Shepherds. The other three are the Tervuren, Laekenois, and Groenendael. In some countries, all four varieties of shepherd are known collectively as the Belgian Sheepdog and are registered as such, but in America, the Malinois has been registered separately from the other varieties since 1959. The name "Malinois" comes from the city of Malines in northwestern Belgium, where the breed originated.

Photo Courtesy of Jacalyn Honeywell

The main differences between the different varieties of Belgian Shepherd are the coat types and colors. The Malinois is a short-coated breed that is typically some shade of fawn with a black mask. The Tervuren is longhaired and ranges in color from fawn to deep mahogany with a black mask. The hairs of the Tervuren are tipped with black, and coats often darken with age. Other colors do exist but are not standard. The Groenendael is a long-haired dog that is always black. White toe tips are acceptable, but large patches of white are not. The fourth variety of Shepherd, the Laekenois, possesses a wiry, curly coat and ranges in color from fawn to mahogany to red sable, all with some blackening around the muzzle and tail.

Originally developed to herd livestock, the four varieties of Belgian Shepherd were the result of breeders favoring the dog's abilities over appearance, but eventually it was decided that a standard needed to be developed to guide the breeders toward their ideal dog. In 1891, Belgian veterinarian Adolphe Reul gathered a group of Belgian Shepherd breeders and recommended that they only breed their dogs to others of the same coat type, no matter what color their coat was. Nearly all of the breeders agreed. By April 3, 1892, the Belgian Shepherd Breed Club had been

Photo Courtesy of Jordan Cook

developed and the first detailed breed standard was drawn up.

In 1901, the Societie Royal Saint Hubert was the first organization to recognize the Belgian Shepherd as a single breed with four varieties. By about 1910 the type and temperament of the Belgian Shepherd had been established. This was something breeders could agree on, though there were still many disagreements on coat type and color.

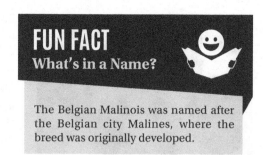

FUN FACT

What's in a Name?

The Belgian Malinois was named after the Belgian city Malines, where the breed was originally developed.

After the start of World War I, the breed's population was reduced, and efforts were made to save it from extinction. Regulations were adjusted so that quality dogs could be bred, regardless of coat type and color. The different varieties were allowed to interbreed, which meant multiple varieties could be present in a single litter. Puppies were registered according to the variety they were born as, rather than the variety of their parents. In Europe, this registration practice still exists.

The Belgian Malinois eventually made its way to America and was recognized by the American Kennel Club in 1911. However, it wasn't until 1959 that the Belgian Shepherd was separated into different breeds. The Malinois and Tervuren kept their names, but the Groenendael was renamed the Belgian Sheepdog. The Laekenois was dropped from recognition. Between 1950 and 1965 the Malinois was exhibited in the Miscellaneous Class, then was moved to the Working Group in 1965. The breed remained there until 1983, when it was decided that the Herding Group was a more appropriate category for the dogs.

The Belgian Malinois in the Military and Police

The breed's versatility and high work drive led to the Malinois being used in World War I as Red Cross messengers and assistants, pulling ambulance carts and carts used to transport firearms and ammunition. Today, the Belgian Malinois can be found working alongside soldiers and military personnel around the world.

Belgian Malinois are the breed of choice for military operations for a variety of reasons, including their size and bravery. Malinois are favored over German Shepherds in operations that involve skydiving due to the fact that Malinois are lighter and easier to strap to their handler's backs. Many Malinois are also trained to skydive by themselves, which is ideal for water landings as skydiving separately is safer for both dog and handler. The Malinois' size allows it to be picked up by its handler when necessary, but the dog is still large enough to be able to control

Photo Courtesy of David Bunney

human aggressors. The breed is also less prone to heat stroke due to their shorter coats and neutral coloring.

The first mention of Belgian Malinois being used by police forces in the United States occurred in New York City in January 1908. That month's issue of the AKC Gazette announced that five Belgian Shepherds had been added to the New York City police force. At that time, the breed was relatively unknown in the US and this notice marked the first mention of the breed by the AKC.

The Belgian Malinois breed is so highly regarded among military K-9s that the memorial to military dogs in Fayetteville, North Carolina, features a true to size bronze statue of a vigilant Malinois in full deployment kit. His ears are pricked, and, in sitting position, he appears ready to receive his next command at any moment. The statue was created by Salt Lake City artist Lena Toritch as a memorial for Special Operations Force K9s that have perished in the line of duty. Each dog lost in combat has its name placed at the base of the bronze statue. In addition to each dog's name, the year and theater of operations where the dog lost its life are also listed.

One of the more well-known Belgian Malinois is Cairo, who played a critical role alongside Seal Team Six in taking down notorious terrorist Osama Bin Laden in 2011. This canine hero was brought along on the mission to sniff out explosives and protect his team from enemies. Afterward, Time magazine awarded Cairo with its prestigious Animal of the Year award. Cairo eventually retired from military work to live comfortably with his handler's family, reportedly helping to carry groceries.

Belgian Malinois are also used as anti-poaching dogs in wildlife parks throughout Africa. They track and apprehend poachers illegally hunting endangered animals within the park's boundaries. In Kruger National Park, officials claim that in the space of about a year, the dogs were responsible for about 168 out of 200 arrests. One Malinois employed by the park, Killer, was involved in the arrests of more than 100 poachers. He was awarded the People's Dispensary for Sick Animals (PDSA) Gold Medal for his efforts. Park officials have described the dogs as game changers in the battle against poachers.

The Modern Belgian Malinois

The modern Belgian Malinois is a versatile breed that excels in nearly every imaginable sport. Different lines of Malinois have resulted in a breed that is capable of succeeding in a variety of dog sports, as well as maintaining its position as a popular family companion. These dogs are ideal for active families and those interested in competing in modern dog sports. The breed is most well-known for its success in protection sports such as French Ring and IPO, but Malinois have also earned titles in obedience, agility, dock diving, herding, and trick dog competitions.

Although the Belgian Malinois is a popular choice for competitors and families alike, it has maintained its natural suspicion toward strangers and will readily protect its family from any perceived threat. This suspicion is natural to many herding breeds but can result in behavioral problems if proper training and socialization does not occur. Additionally, some lines of Malinois possess a strong prey drive and especially high energy level, which can result in a dog that is difficult to handle by inexperienced owners. However, in the right hands, the Belgian Malinois is an affectionate, devoted, and playful companion.

CHAPTER 2
The Belgian Malinois

"If a German Shepherd is a station wagon, then a Malinois is a Corvette. They like to run, be with you, do agility, scent work, and protection work. The key to harnessing their abilities is clear communication and direction, which is all based on the bond you have with them. With the Malinois, the BOND is very important."

ANTHONY RICHLING
Liberty Dog Camp or Liberty K9

Photo Courtesy of
Susie Williamson
Merson Belgian Malinois

Physical Characteristics

The American Kennel Club's standard for the Belgian Malinois describes the breed as a well-balanced and square dog. It is a medium to large breed with a strong and agile appearance. This is a breed with distinct differences between the two genders. Male Belgian Malinois are typically more mas-

FUN FACT
Herding Masters

While the Belgian Malinois is now most often seen doing military or police work, the breed was initially developed to herd sheep.

culine in appearance than their distinctly feminine counterparts. Males are typically between 24 and 26 inches in height, while females are 22 to 24 inches at the withers. Males under 23 inches or over 27 inches at the shoulder will be disqualified from the show ring. This rule also applies to female Belgian Malinois under 21 inches or over 25 inches. At maturity, the breed typically weighs anywhere between 55 and 75 pounds, with females weighing less than males. The bone structure should appear strong and sturdy, but neither bulky and cumbersome nor spindly and leggy.

The head of the Belgian Malinois should be in proportion to the body. The eyes are brown, medium sized, and almond shaped. They should give the impression of alertness, intelligence, and readiness for activity. The rims of the eyes should always be black. The ears of the Malinois are in the shape of an equilateral triangle. They are stiff, erect, and in proportion to the size of the dog's skull. Hanging ears or semi-prick ears are considered a disqualification in the show ring. The dog's muzzle is pointed, but not snipy, and equal in length to the skull itself. The Belgian Malinois should have powerful jaws with teeth that meet in a scissor or level bite. The lips should always be tight and black, with no pink showing. Overshot and undershot bites are faulted, as are missing teeth.

The Belgian Malinois' neck should be long enough to permit the head to be carried proudly. It should slope smoothly into the dog's level topline. The body should appear powerful without bulkiness. The chest is deep, but not broad, reaching to the dog's elbow. The front legs are muscular and parallel. The paws of the Malinois are round and tight, resembling those of a cat. They may or may not have dewclaws. The nails should always be black except where there are white toe tips. The hindquarters of the Belgian Malinois should appear balanced with the forequarters and equal in strength. The hind legs should be well-angled, but not in a way that resembles the angulation of a German Shepherd. The legs should be parallel and in proportion to the overall size of the dog. For conformation competition, any hind dewclaws should be removed.

Photo Courtesy of
Edgar Frias Carrasco

The coat of the Belgian Malinois should be short, straight, and weather-resistant. A dense undercoat should be present. The hair on the head, ears, and lower legs is shorter than the hair covering the majority of the body. Around the neck, and on the tail and back of the thighs, the hair is permitted to be somewhat longer, but should not stand out too far or hang down. The coat may vary in color from rich fawn to dark mahogany with a black mask and ears. The underparts of the dog are allowed to be a lighter fawn, but lighter coloring on the body is considered a fault in the show ring. Malinois are allowed to have white toe tips as well as a small white spot on the breastbone, but no other white markings are permitted. Though color is important to the breed, temperament and structure should take precedence in judging.

The Belgian Malinois' gait should appear free and easy with front and hind legs converging toward the center line of gravity. The topline should always remain firm and level. Belgian Malinois display a marked tendency to move in a circular motion rather than in a straight line if given the option. This breed is known for its high energy and endurance, so the dog's movement should reflect its seemingly inexhaustible nature.

Behavioral Characteristics

"As with any breed, there is a spectrum of temperaments within the Belgian Malinois breed. I find this to be especially true in working type breeds. The attributes exhibited from a working line Malinois will vary greatly based on a number of factors including: lineage, country of origin, influence of dog sport, type of pedigree(x-Malinois vs. FCI Malinois), objective of breeding program, etc. That being said, there is no one lifestyle for all Malinois, nor one Malinois for all lifestyles. Generally, an active lifestyle with a handler or family willing to participate in some form of formal training and regular exercise would be well suited for a Malinois."

MARK ROTH JR.
BlackJack Malinois

One of the most notable characteristics of the Belgian Malinois is their astonishing intelligence. In a study performed by renowned behaviorist Stanley Coren, the Belgian Malinois was determined to be the 26th most intelligent dog breed out of the 138 breeds that participated. This ranking rated the breed as excellent working dogs who typically understand new commands after less than fifteen repetitions and obey the first command at least 85% of the time or better. Coren's study defines three aspects of dog intelligence: instinctive intelligence, adaptive intelligence, and working or obedience intelligence. These three aspects refer to a dog's ability to perform the tasks it was bred for, solve problems on its own, and learn from humans. As shown by this study, the Belgian Malinois is a smart and highly trainable breed.

Belgian Malinois should display confidence, even when they are uncertain. If trained and socialized properly, the breed should never be shy or aggressive. In fact, the stable temperament of this breed is so important that any fearful or aggressive behavior is strongly penalized in the show ring.

The Belgian Malinois is also well-known for its strong desire to work. This is a high energy breed that will not be content to sit on the sofa all day. Many experienced Malinois owners have described their dogs as "inexhaustible." However, it's important to note that energy levels can vary among different bloodlines.

Belgian Malinois as Family Dogs

"The Belgian Malinois is best suited for an active family, one that either participates in some type of sport or activity, IE: Schutzhund, SAR, Frisbee, Agility, Dock Diving, Herding, Hiking, or that is very committed to keeping the active, playing ball, long walks sometimes multiple times a day, bike riding with the dog, anything to keep the dogs mind active. A bored Belgian Malinois is usually a destructive Belgian Malinois."

BETH ROOD
Roodhaus Belgian Malinois

The Belgian Malinois is a loyal and affectionate breed that can be a great companion for any active family as long as it receives the right training, exercise, and management. Children and dogs should both be taught how to behave around one another. The same is true for Malinois living with other pets or animals. Some Malinois may have a higher prey drive than others, but if they are socialized well from the start, many Malinois can safely live around a variety of animals. As long as there is mutual respect and plenty of ongoing socialization and training, the Malinois can live comfortably in any family setting.

It should be noted that Belgian Malinois are naturally protective and can be reserved around strangers. They are friendly and loving with their families and those they know well, but they can be cautious around new people. It's unlikely that a Belgian Malinois will run up and greet a stranger in the same manner as a Labrador Retriever. Instead, Malinois are more likely to take their time assessing the situation before they decide whether the stranger is friend or foe. As such, this is a breed that will need lifelong socializing in order to make sure that a dog understands that not all new people are a threat to his loved ones. This does not mean Belgian Malinois are overly aggressive. They simply want to protect their families from any perceived threat and will rarely lash out unless they feel that they have no other option.

Belgian Malinois can be a great addition to an active family, but they are not dogs that can be walked on weekends and left to fend for themselves during the busy weekdays. This is not a breed that can be put out into a backyard and left to exercise itself. Malinois love spending time with their families and a neglectful environment or lack of sufficient exercise is sure to result in behavioral problems.

If you have small children, you might want to reconsider bringing home a Belgian Malinois. While most Malinois will never purposely hurt a child, they can be overly enthusiastic at times, which can result in smaller children being knocked to the ground. Regardless of your children's ages, if you do bring home a Malinois, you should always supervise any interaction between kids and the new dog.

Photo Courtesy of
Kaylin Hall

Photo Courtesy of
Dionne Cancino

Belgian Malinois make great hiking, biking, running, or even swimming companions. If it's an activity where the dog can be involved with the family, your Malinois will gladly join you. The more active your family is, the more content and trainable your Belgian Malinois will be. Remember, a tired dog is a happy dog!

Belgian Malinois as Working Dogs

If you're looking for a working or sport dog, the Belgian Malinois may be just the breed for you. This breed's high energy and incredible intelligence help it excel in a variety of different sports. In fact, dog sports are a great way to make sure that your Belgian Malinois gets the physical and mental exercise he needs each day.

Belgian Malinois are particularly known for their success in protection sports such as IPO, French Ring, and Mondio Ring. If you're unfamiliar with protection sports, Chapter 13 will go into more detail about each of these events and the requirements of each, as well as what titles your dog can earn. Typically, each sport requires a combination of bite work, obedience, and sometimes even tracking. Most of this work is done off leash, so the dog must listen to his handler's every command. To be successful in protection sports, a dog must be athletic, focused, and courageous, which is exactly why Belgian Malinois are one of the most popular choices for competitors.

Belgian Malinois are also known to excel in both competition obedience and agility, as well as dock diving and flyball. Some dogs may also do well in nose work, canicross, or weight pulling. The breed's speed, agility, and intelligence make them highly competitive in any sport they enter. Treibball gives Malinois a chance to express their natural herding instinct without the need for sheep. Conformation competition is another competitive avenue for any Malinois, though it requires less physical action and more mental focus.

The Malinois is a highly adaptable breed that is suited for a variety of sports and occupations. However, it's important to note that there are specific bloodlines within the breed that make certain dogs more suited to one sport than another. Dogs that have been strictly bred for herding may not have the grit required for protection sports. Likewise, a dog bred to excel in protection sports may not have a suitable temperament as a herder. It's crucial to keep this in mind when deciding whether this is the right breed for you and your family.

Photo Courtesy of Grace Santana

Inexperienced Owners Beware

Although the Belgian Malinois is a beautiful, athletic, and capable dog, it's not the right breed for everyone, especially first-time dog owners or families inexperienced with high drive dogs. This is especially true for dogs descending from working bloodlines. These dogs need a considerable amount of physical and mental exercise each and every day. They are not suitable for a couch potato lifestyle. No matter how much you have going on in your life or how tired you are at the end of the day, a Belgian Malinois will still need his walk, run, or play or training session. Belgian Malinois have an extreme work ethic and do not take days off. If a Belgian Malinois does not receive enough physical or mental stimulation, behavioral problems are sure to develop. This can include destructive behavior such as chewing, digging, or relieving himself in the house. It can also include behaviors such as incessant barking, escaping, and aggression. It's essential that you understand how much work it takes to keep a Malinois content before you bring home a new puppy.

Unless you are an experienced Malinois owner, it's also important that you research the right bloodlines and connect with the right breeder. Finding the right dog for your lifestyle is necessary to set your relationship up for success. Of course, this isn't always possible with rescue dogs, but it's still important to know what type of dog you're looking for so you don't end up with more dog than you can handle.

CHAPTER 3
Where to Find Your Belgian Malinois

"If you are considering a Malinois for your family, you need to visit or talk to as many breeders and rescue people as you can. Visit litters and adults before you are ready for a puppy. The American Kennel Club also sponsors 'Meet the Breed' events, or find performance shows in your area, or training clubs to attend and talk to people about the breed. Get some hands on time before bringing home your puppy or adult dog."

JANET WOLFF
Stahlrosenhof Intl K-9

Photo Courtesy of
Chynna Crawford

Adopting an Adult vs. Puppy

Before you begin your search for a Belgian Malinois, you'll need to decide if you would prefer to bring home a puppy or an adult dog. Both options have pros and cons, but you'll need to carefully consider your options so that you can make the right decision for you and your family.

Most importantly, you'll need to consider the purpose of your new dog. Are you looking for a competition or show dog, or an active family companion? If

HELPFUL TIP
Rescue

Belgian Malinois are great dogs, but they aren't right for everybody. Sadly, many people underestimate just how much exercise, attention, and training this breed needs. As a result, Mals tend to end up in rescues and shelters. Consider rescuing your Belgian Malinois rather than buying a puppy. You'll be saving two lives; the dog you rescue and the dog whose spot is opened up by getting a dog out of the shelter or rescue.

you're interested in competing with your new Belgian Malinois in specific sports, you may prefer a puppy so that you can train the dog any way you like. However, if you're just looking for a new family member or would prefer a dog with a little training, an adult might suit your household better. Whether you've committed to buying from a breeder or adopting from a shelter, you should be able to find both puppies and adults available. Breeders often have retired show or breeding dogs that need a new home, while shelters get puppies in fairly frequently.

In addition to being able to train a puppy yourself, you also have the benefit of bringing home a dog with no prior behavioral problems. With a puppy, you're essentially starting with a blank slate. You won't have to deal with any issues that were developed in previous homes. You'll be able to socialize a puppy the way you want in order to ensure that your new dog will get along with all of your family members, whether human or animal. Additionally, choosing a puppy gives you the option of buying a dog that has been bred specifically for what you want to do with it. For example, you can choose a puppy from a breeder known for success in the conformation ring or a breeder that has won numerous titles in protection sports.

However, bringing home a puppy is a huge responsibility. You'll need to deal with housetraining, teething, and training from scratch. This means that any behavioral problems that develop will be on you. You'll need to make sure you're socializing your puppy correctly from the very beginning while still making sure he's protected if he hasn't yet had all his vaccines. A Belgian Malinois puppy is a lot of work, so you need to make sure that you and all your family members are prepared for this commitment.

Photo Courtesy of Nyla and Patrick Dodds

If a puppy sounds like a lot of work, you might want to consider bringing home an adult. With adult dogs, you have the benefit of not having to deal with the chewing associated with teething and it's likely the dog has already been housetrained. He may even know a handful of commands already as well as the basic rules of living in a house. You'll also be able to dive right into sport training or athletic activities as you won't need to worry about harming your dog's developing body.

This does not mean that you won't face challenges by bringing home an adult Belgian Malinois. Although many adult dogs are relatively well trained with few behavioral problems, you may be looking at a dog who has had bad experiences in a previous home. He may or may not be housetrained and could have behavioral problems. It's important to find out why the dog needs a new home, as it may act aggressively toward cats or children. Housetraining an adult dog can be somewhat more difficult as you'll be retraining the dog, rather than teaching him something new. Before you bring home your new Belgian Malinois, try to picture your ideal dog, so you'll have a better idea of what you're looking for and where to find it.

Purchasing from a Breeder vs. Adopting from a Shelter

If you've already decided whether you're bringing home a puppy or an adult Belgian Malinois, you'll then need to decide where you plan to adopt your new dog from. Again, knowing the reason behind your desire to bring a new dog into your home will help you make your decision. If you're planning on competing at the highest levels of dog sports, you'll prob-ably want to adopt a dog from a breeder that's familiar with those

HELPFUL TIP
Avoid Backyard Breeders

As the Belgian Malinois is becoming increasingly popular, unscrupulous breeders are popping up and breed-ing Mals with no regard for the health of the breed. Do your research to make sure you're getting your puppy from a reputable breeder who does health test-ing to ensure they're only breeding the healthiest dogs

sports. That's not to say that a shelter dog won't be successful, but it will stack the odds in your favor. On the other hand, if you're just looking for an active and affectionate family member, you can choose between finding the right breeder or adopting from a shelter or rescue organization. No matter where you choose to find your Belgian Malinois, it's important to remember that you may have the option of choosing an adult or puppy from either a breeder or a rescue.

One of the benefits of buying a Belgian Malinois from a breeder is the breed-er's knowledge and experience with the breed. Not only will a reputable breeder produce healthy, high quality dogs, but he or she will also be aware of health and behavioral problems that are common to the breed. Reputable breeders will also be willing to provide support throughout the dog's life as needed. This level of support may range from answering any questions you may have to mentoring you in dog sports. Additionally, breeders know their dogs, their bloodlines, and what they are capable of. You'll be able to buy a dog with the confidence that you know what you're getting. This is especially important if you intend to show or compete with your new dog.

However, there are also some drawbacks to buying a Malinois from a breeder. The purchase price will be significantly higher than the adoption fee of a dog from a rescue organization. Additionally, you'll be responsible for initial veterinary fees for vaccines, deworming, and spaying or neutering. Buying from a breeder also means you won't be rescuing a dog that is desperately in need of a home. Many owners of rescue dogs report a feeling of satisfaction from knowing that they gave a shelter dog the opportunity for a better life.

As mentioned, adopting a Belgian Malinois from a shelter or rescue organization does often mean lower adoption fees as well as the benefit of bringing home a fully vaccinated and spayed or neutered dog. However, it's important to understand that dogs do end up in shelters for reasons other than a family simply not being able to afford the dog anymore. There are dogs in rescue that have been neglected, abused, or have developed difficult health or behavioral problems. Obviously, this is not true of all rescue dogs, but it is important to keep in mind when considering a rescue dog.

Rescuing a Belgian Malinois

If you plan on adopting your new Belgian Malinois from a shelter or rescue organization, rather than buying from a breeder, it's still crucial that you have an idea of what you're looking for in your new family member. You'll also need to decide on what your deal breakers are, such as whether you're willing to take on a dog with special needs. Most behavioral problems can be overcome with patience and training, and many health issues can be managed with proper veterinary care. However, if you have other pets or children in your home, you may not be willing to work with a dog that has a history of displaying aggressive behavior. On the other hand, if you live in the right kind of household, that may be exactly the challenge you're looking for.

If you have kids or other pets, not only will you need to discuss them with the rescue staff or volunteers, but you'll also need to introduce them to any dog that you're considering adopting. Generally, an introduction is required by the shelter or rescue before the dog can leave the facility or foster home. This requirement is for the safety of the dog as well as the safety of your human and animal family members.

Some rescue organizations may also require a home check before allowing you to take home your new dog. A home check typically consists of a volunteer or staff member visiting your home to make sure it's a safe environment for a new dog. They'll check to make sure your yard is fully fenced and that there are no significant risks to any pets in the home. Often, if they find any minor problems, such as a hole in the fence, they're willing to give you a chance to fix it instead of denying your application. It can be nerve-wracking to have someone come to examine your home, but rest assured, they are only making sure it's safe and aren't there to make judgments about your décor.

*Photo Courtesy of
Susie Williamson
Merson Belgian Malinois*

Questions to Ask Before Bringing a Belgian Malinois Home

The more questions you ask a breeder or shelter staff member, the more confident you can be that you're bringing home the right dog for your family and lifestyle. Be sure to ask plenty of questions about the dog's history and health status. There are specific questions you should ask depending on the age of the dog you're adopting. Some questions may be more appropriate for dogs coming from breeders while others are best suited for dogs being adopted from a shelter or rescue. Here are a few age-appropriate questions to ask before committing to a Belgian Malinois:

When Adopting an Adult Dog

- How does he/she get along with other dogs?
- Has the dog received all necessary vaccines?
- Is he/she spayed or neutered?
- Is the dog friendly with children?
- Does the dog have any health or behavioral problems?
- Does the dog display any food aggression or resource guarding?
- Has the dog been introduced to cats/horses/etc.?
- Does the dog play well with other dogs?
- What commands does the dog already know?
- What kind of food is the dog currently eating?
- After describing my ideal dog, does this dog seem like a good match?

When Adopting a Puppy

- Have the parents been health tested?
- If so, may I see the test results?
- What age-appropriate vaccines has the puppy received?
- Can the puppy be registered with the AKC or another kennel club?
- What is the puppy's personality like so far?
- How likely is the puppy to succeed in the sport of my choice?
- Have the puppy's parents competed in the sport of my choice?
- What type of food has the puppy been weaned onto?
- After describing my ideal dog, does this puppy seem like a good match?

Choosing a Reputable Breeder

"Ask about the puppies parents: Are they show or working lines? Ask about their grandparents too. Try and get as much background as possible if going with a rescue. Even within the breed itself some lines are way more 'energetic' than others. Do not go by how they look."

ANTHONY RICHLING

Liberty Dog Camp or Liberty K9

It can be challenging to connect with the right breeder, but there are plenty of resources to help you find the dog of your dreams. It's essential that you research Belgian Malinois breeders and find a reputable breeder instead of buying the first puppy you find. Buying a Malinois from a reputable breeder will ensure that you're getting the healthiest puppy possible with the best chance of success, in either the show ring or your home.

Try attending a few local dog shows or competitions, or contact local dog sports clubs. Competitors and club members are usually happy to discuss their dogs and where they came from. This will also give you a chance to see what type of dogs a breeder is producing and decide whether you think they would be ideal for you. The people who are actively involved in the breed may also be able to steer you away from less reputable breeders in the area.

If you live in an area with limited opportunities to discuss the topic with local enthusiasts, you can also search the internet for breeders. As with everything on the internet, it's important to scrutinize the information you read and not take everything at face value. A backyard breeder may have a nicer website than one of the top breeders in the country, but if they can't guarantee the health of their puppies, you should probably avoid them. Most reputable breeders keep their sites updated with performance records, health test results, photos, and any upcoming or expected litters. You should also be able to find their contact information so you can have a conversation with them via phone or email.

Reputable breeders will never have anything to hide. Most breeders are happy to discuss their dogs in depth and want to know as much about you as you do about them. They would rather guide you toward the right dog for your situation than push whatever puppies they have left. Most breeders will also welcome you into their home to meet their breeds. One exception to this is if they have particularly young puppies and want to limit the puppies' exposure to any potential outside infection. However, if you suspect that the person you're talking to isn't telling you the truth, or is trying to hide something, you should keep looking.

Contracts and Guarantees

Typically, reputable breeders will require you to sign a contract before allowing you to put a deposit down on a puppy or adult Belgian Malinois. The puppy you're buying may look healthy at first glance, but a contract typically contains a health guarantee that ensures that the puppy is in top health on the day it leaves the breeder's home. It may also state what vaccinations the puppy has had and what health testing has been done to the parents.

A breeder's contract is intended to protect both you and the breeder should something go wrong with the purchase. Often, by signing a contract you are agreeing to the breeder's terms of adoption. This may mean spaying or neutering at an appropriate age, providing the dog with appropriate veterinary care, and returning the dog to the breeder should you no longer be able to care for it. Certain breeders, especially those that feed raw diets, may also require you to feed the puppy a certain way.

Remember, the contract is a legally binding document, so you need to read it thoroughly before signing. If you have any questions or concerns regarding the content of the document, be sure to discuss them with the breeder before picking up a pen. Some breeders may be willing to change certain clauses within the document under certain circumstances, but it's important to only sign the contract if you agree to everything contained within.

Health Testing and Certifications

"When purchasing a Belgian Malinois from a breeder, be sure to ask for references from past owners of their dogs. Also check out the breeder's dogs at the Orthopedic Foundation for Animals website - www.ofa.org - to make sure their breeding dogs have passing hips, elbows and eyes at minimum. If a breeder makes excuses or balks at answering the health questions on their dogs, please say goodbye and go to another breeder!"

SUSIE WILLIAMSON
Merson Belgian Malinois

Reputable breeders are always trying to improve their breed with every generation. To accomplish this, they implement stringent breeding practices and only dogs who have satisfactory results in all required health testing can be bred, so as to limit health problems in future generations. The most common organization used to test potential breeding dogs is the Orthopedic Foundation for Animals (OFA).

The OFA is one of the leading organizations in canine genetic research. Their database contains results from thousands of individual dogs of nearly every recognized breed. Breeders and owners can have their dogs tested by local veterinarians or laboratories and have the results sent to the OFA for examination for a nominal fee. Most tests require that a dog be at least 12 months of age at the time of testing, but some tests may need to be performed at a younger or

Photo Courtesy of Rachel Oscherwitz

older age. The OFA's website has a list of recommended tests for each breed and what age they should be performed.

For Belgian Malinois, the OFA recommends testing for both hip and elbow dysplasia. In order for the results to be recorded, dogs must be at least 24 months of age at the time of testing. The dog must also undergo an annual eye examination by an ophthalmologist boarded by the American College of Veterinary Ophthalmologists. Additionally, dogs must be permanently identified by either a microchip or tattoo. Once all of these requirements are met, the dog's results are submitted to the OFA's Canine Health Information Center (CHIC) and are made publicly available on the OFA's website.

Adopting an Adult Dog

Many adult dogs find themselves in a rescue or shelter environment through no fault of their own. Perhaps their previous owner passed away or their family could no longer afford them. However, some may have been given up for behavioral reasons, such as aggression toward another pet. It's important to get to know the dog you're considering adopting as well as you can before bringing him home. The more you know about him, the better prepared you'll be when you run into problems.

It's important to consider that unless you're adopting a dog that has been in a foster home, his personality in the hectic shelter environment may be different from the way he behaves in a home environment. Shelters are typically loud, chaotic, and stressful, which may impact the way your new Belgian Malinois acts. He may seem timid or bark excessively. In these situations, you may not be able to get to know the dog well until you get him home and spend more time with him one-on-one.

Likewise, you may also find that as your new dog becomes more comfortable in your home, he becomes bolder about engaging in inappropriate behavior. The stress of changing environments can sometimes cause dogs to shut down temporarily, but they will eventually come out of their shell as they become more confident that they won't be shuffled around to a new home or shelter. It's crucial that you and all of your family members are prepared to deal with any unexpected behaviors with consistency and patience. Remember, this is a new experience for your Belgian Malinois, too.

How to Choose Your Ideal Dog

"Look for a dog with the temperament, personality and energy level that fits your situation. If you are more of a homebody you don't want the dog that is high drive and high energy, you want a dog that is low key and has what we call an "off switch" meaning it knows how to relax and lay around the house. If you are a high energy person who is always moving, you like to run or bike, you have weekends and evenings free you would probably be a good fit for that high energy dog that needs someone to run with and play ball, and do activities on the nights and weekends."

BETH ROOD
Roodhaus Belgian Malinois

When picking out your ideal Belgian Malinois it's important that you focus more on the dog's temperament and athletic ability than his appearance. While it can be easy to get caught up in the Malinois' graceful and majestic appearance, choosing a dog that's right for you and your lifestyle is more important than your favorite coat color.

It can be helpful to make a list of your ideal traits before you begin your search. If you know what type of personality you're looking for, you'll be less likely to get caught up on looks when you're presented with a litter of adorable puppies. Do you want an outgoing dog or one that's more reserved? Are you looking for a future athlete or show ring star? The more thoroughly you consider your ideal dog, the better you can explain to the breeder or shelter staff what you're looking for.

Additionally, you should always consider the breeder or rescue staff's opinion. They know their dogs better than you do, so if they think a certain dog would suit you best, you should consider it. Reputable breeders will not hesitate to let you know if the dog of your choice isn't the best choice for you, so you need to listen to them. They often have years of experience with matching the right dogs to the right families.

Finally, you need to listen to your instincts. If you have doubts about whether an individual dog is right for you, take some time to think about it before committing. It can be easy to get pressured into agreeing to a dog when it's right in front of you and your kids are begging, but bringing a Belgian Malinois home is a huge responsibility so you need to be certain that you're making the right choice. Most breeders will happily give you time to think about it. Many rescue organizations or shelters will also be happy to give you time to consider as they want what's best for the dogs in their care.

CHAPTER 4
Preparing Your Family for a Belgian Malinois

"It is not enough for a Malinois to have an active family. Everyone in the family must be willing to participate in the dog's care and training. A family must be willing to provide outlets for their high energy as well as mental stimulation."

JANET WOLFF
Stahlrosenhof Intl K-9

Photo Courtesy of
Anne-Marie Stoltz

Yearly Costs of Owning a Belgian Malinois

Before you bring your new Belgian Malinois home, you need to consider the yearly cost of dog ownership. If you're living on a particularly tight budget, you may need to reconsider bringing a dog into your home at this time. In most cases dog ownership is possible with proper planning and preparation.

One of the first costs of dog ownership that you'll encounter is the adoption fee or purchase price. If you're adopting your

FUN FACT
Belgian Sheepdogs

Outside the United States, the four Belgian Shepherd dog breeds — the Malinois, Tervuren, Groenendael, and Laekenois — are all considered different varieties of the same breed. The AKC recognizes the four types as separate breeds. The four dogs have similar builds and temperaments, but they have four very different coat types and colorations.

Belgian Malinois from a shelter or rescue organization, you'll probably need to pay a fee. The fee typically ranges from $50 to $450 or more, depending on the area you live in and the organization you're adopting from. Since most rescues require dogs to be spayed or neutered and fully vaccinated prior to adoption, your fee will go toward covering those costs.

If you're purchasing your Belgian Malinois from a breeder, the initial cost is going to be much higher. The average price for a Malinois is about $1,100 but a dog from a reputable breeder can easily cost up to $3,500. Dogs from top sport bloodlines can even cost upwards of $9,000. The price of your new puppy will vary according to what health tests have been done by the breeder, the parents' performance records, as well as the potential of the individual puppy. Unlike shelter dogs, vaccines and spaying or neutering are not usually covered in this cost. Puppies may have at least one round of vaccines and deworming, but adults may have more.

As intimidating as these costs may seem, the initial cost of your new Belgian Malinois will be the least of your financial concerns. Supplies and routine veterinary care are not optional, and costs can add up quickly. Depending on where you live and the quality of the food and supplies you buy, you may be looking at between $1,065 and $3,810 or more for the first year of ownership.

Here is a breakdown of the potential costs you will face in the first year of dog ownership:

Mandatory Expenses	Cost Estimate
Food	$300 - $900
Food and Water Dishes	$10 - $50
Treats	$50 - $150
Toys	$20 - $100
Collars and Leashes	$10 - $100
Crate	$50 - $200
Dog Beds	$50 - $350
Vaccines and Routine Veterinary Care	$150 - $500
Heartworm Testing	$10 - $35
Heartworm Prevention	$25 - $125
Flea and Tick Prevention	$40 - $200
Spaying and Neutering	$150 - $600
Puppy Classes	$200 - $500
Total	**$1,065 - $3,810**

Unfortunately, those are not the only costs you'll need to consider. Although Belgian Malinois are relatively low maintenance in terms of grooming, you'll still need to budget long-term for grooming services if you don't plan on grooming your dog yourself. Grooming prices will vary according to where you live, but you should be prepared to spend somewhere between $35 and $70 each time you take your Malinois to the groomer.

Unless you plan on taking your Belgian Malinois with you when you travel, you'll also need to budget for the cost of a pet sitter or boarding kennel. Again, this cost will vary according your area and the quality of care provided, but you may be looking at upwards of $50 per day. Of course, the best option is to seek the help of dog-loving friends and family that can look after your Malinois while you're away.

The most significant potential cost you'll face in dog ownership is emergency veterinary services. Of course, you'll always do your best to keep your Malinois as healthy as possible, but accidents can and do happen. Emergency care can range from just a few hundred dollars for minor procedures to several thousand dollars, especially if your dog requires emergency surgery or hospitalization. Although pet insurance is an option, many owners choose to set aside money on a regular basis to help cover the cost of emergencies when they arise.

Photo Courtesy of
Michael DeLosSantos

Possible Expenses	Cost Estimate
Professional Grooming	$100 - $500+
Emergency Veterinary Services	$200 - $2000+
Pet Sitting or Boarding	$15 - $80+ per day

It's important to note that this section is not intended to frighten you away from bringing a Belgian Malinois into your home. It's simply meant to prepare you for the potential financial burden of dog ownership. Bringing an animal into your home is a huge responsibility that should not be taken lightly. With careful planning and budgeting, you'll be able to provide your Malinois with the best care that you can afford without putting unnecessary strain on your finances.

Preparing Children

Before you commit to bringing home a Belgian Malinois, it's important that you sit down with your children and discuss their potential new family member. It may seem tempting to surprise your children with an adorable puppy, but it will be better for both the puppy and the children if they are prepared for such an event. They may get too excited in the moment and may accidentally overwhelm or frighten the new dog. It's not uncommon for scared dogs to lash out, so to prevent your children from being bitten, it's best to talk about the new dog and how to behave around him.

First, you'll want to explain to them how to interact with a new dog. Regardless of whether you're bringing home an adult or a puppy, it's essential that the children remain calm around the new dog. Elevated emotions this early in the relationship can set things off to a bad start. Instead, ask them to sit or stand quietly and allow the dog to approach them. Encourage them to let the dog sniff them before attempting to pet the dog. With puppies, it may be easier for the children to sit on the floor, so they aren't towering over a nervous puppy. Most importantly, children should never be allowed to pick up a puppy. Even a small fall from a child's arms can be enough to seriously injure a puppy.

If your kids are old enough, you might also want to discuss their responsibilities with the new dog. If you intend to assign them certain chores, such as feeding or cleaning up after the puppy, now is the time to prepare them. It can be empowering to give children some responsibility in caring for a pet, so don't be afraid to let them help when possible. Just remember that some supervision will be necessary.

Photo Courtesy of
Coco Marin

Finally, you'll need to determine the rules of the house and discuss them with the kids prior to the new dog's arrival. If you intend to keep the new dog off the furniture, or discourage him from jumping on people, now is the time to introduce those rules to your children. The more consistently these rules are enforced from the moment your new Belgian Malinois comes home, the more quickly he'll learn how to behave in his new home.

Preparing Your Other Pets

Depending on the type of pets you have, you'll need to be careful about introducing your new Belgian Malinois to your existing household. Chapter 11 discusses proper introductions with multi-pet households in more detail. Whether you're introducing a puppy or adult dog into your household, patience is key. You'll also need to make sure that all pets are allowed to have a safe space to retreat to if they feel uncomfortable or overwhelmed.

If you have other dogs, you may also want to buy new toys or beds for the new arrival. Some dogs, especially older dogs, may be reluctant to share their beloved possessions with a new dog. This does not mean you should allow your current dogs to exhibit resource-guarding behaviors, it's just meant to discourage disagreements.

Family Commitment

Remember, bringing a new dog into your household is a huge commitment. Before bringing your Belgian Malinois home, you need to make sure that everyone is in agreement. If your family doesn't entirely agree to this commitment, you may need to reconsider. If everyone does agree, you'll need to make sure that all family members are thoroughly prepared for the new arrival and know their role in his care.

It can be helpful to hold a family meeting prior to the decision to adopt a new dog and again prior to his arrival. During these discussions, you can make sure that everyone agrees not only to the new dog, but to his ongoing care. Each family member can be assigned a role in the new dog's care, if necessary. It can be helpful to have everyone make a list of their desired traits in the new dog and their desired roles in his care, as well as any concerns they may have. This way, every member of your family will be on the same page when the new dog arrives.

CHAPTER 5
Preparing Your Home for Your New Belgian Malinois

Creating a Safe Area Indoors

Before you bring your new Belgian Malinois home for the first time, you want to make sure your home is a safe and comfortable space. Even if you have other pets in your home, you'll still need to do some puppy-proofing to make sure your new family member stays out of trouble. Part of ensuring your new dog's safety is setting up a secure area for him to retreat to when he is feeling overwhelmed or you're unable to supervise.

Many new dog owners choose to set up their new companion's area in a laundry room, guest bathroom, or part of the kitchen. Smaller spaces are ideal for puppies or adults that are not yet housetrained. Dogs don't like to relieve themselves too closely to their sleeping or eating areas, so the smaller the space, the more quickly housetraining will progress. Regardless of the size of the room or space, you'll want to choose a room with easy to clean floors such as tile or linoleum. During the first few weeks or months with your new Belgian Malinois, you're guaranteed to have a few messes to clean up, so try to avoid carpeted areas if possible. It's also best to choose an area that is out of the way, but not secluded. If your new dog is able to watch the everyday activities of your family from the safety of his own space, he'll still feel included but won't be underfoot.

After you've decided where your Malinois is going to stay, you'll need to determine how to secure the area. Belgian Malinois are clever dogs that can quickly figure their way out of an area if given the opportunity, so you'll need to make sure there's no way your new dog can jump out or otherwise escape. Flimsy baby gates or standing barriers are no match for a Malinois' athleticism and determination, so you may need to get creative. If you're bringing home a puppy, a sturdy pressure-mounted baby gate should be enough to contain the puppy, at least for a few months. If you're bringing home an adult Malinois, you may need to consider taller barriers, playpens, or a heavy-duty crate. No matter what type of barrier you choose to use, make sure it's installed properly to prevent escape or injury to your new companion and unnecessary damage to your home.

Photo Courtesy of
Harley Tamm

Crates and Crate Training

"I highly recommend crate training all Belgian Malinois from the time they are puppies. This makes for them less likely to destroy crates and be crate escapers. Once a Belgian Malinois starts destroying crates it is almost impossible to stop them and there is only a handful of crates on the market, expensive crates, that will hold them in safely."

BETH ROOD
Roodhaus Belgian Malinois

Whether you're bringing home a puppy or an adult Belgian Malinois, crate training is a crucial part of your dog's education. Even if you don't plan on crating your dog after he's fully housetrained, it's still an important skill that he will need to know as he will likely spend time in a crate at the groomer or vet.

Dogs that have not been properly crate trained frequently panic once the door is shut behind them. Instead of entering the crate on their own, they often have to be forced inside, which can be quite difficult with a powerful dog such as the Belgian Malinois. Incessant barking and digging or chewing at the crate walls

Photo Courtesy of
Michael DeLosSantos

Photo Courtesy of
Marsha Esslinger

and door are common behaviors in dogs with little to no crate training. Not only is this experience unnecessarily stressful for your dog and those around him, but he can become seriously injured. He may injure his paws, nails, or teeth in his attempts to escape the crate. Rather than put your dog through this unpleasant experience should he ever need to spend time in a crate, it's best to start training him correctly from the start.

Eventually, your Malinois will see the crate not as a prison, but as a comfortable place that he can retreat to when he needs a break. Many dogs come to see their crates as a safe haven, both at home and on the road. Crates can become a portable source of comfort for your dog, so if you travel frequently, a crate can provide your dog with a sense of security no matter whether you're staying at a hotel on vacation or are attending a dog show on the other side of the country.

You'll need to decide what type of crate you'd like to use for your Belgian Malinois. Crates are available in a wide variety of materials including metal, wood, and plastic. Some are more decorative, while others are meant to withstand more destructive dogs. As you can imagine, the cost of these crates will vary greatly. Plastic crates, such as those used for air travel, and metal wire crates tend to be the most budget-friendly, while stylish wooden or heavy-duty metal crates will cost more.

It's essential that the crate you choose is an appropriate size for your dog, which can be somewhat difficult with growing puppies. You want the crate to be large enough for your Malinois to stand up, turn around, and lie down comfortably, but not so large that he feels compelled to use one corner of the crate as a bathroom. For puppies, this may mean changing crate sizes until they reach maturity or using a crate with a movable divider to adjust the size of the available space as needed.

Photo Courtesy of
Caitlyn Lawing

Once you've purchased your new companion's crate, you'll want to make it as appealing as possible to encourage him to willingly spend time inside. Try placing his favorite bed, blanket, or toy inside. Supervision is crucial at first if you plan on leaving your dog with items inside his crate. If he begins to chew or destroy his bedding or toys, you'll need to remove them immediately to prevent him from swallowing or choking on any of the pieces.

HELPFUL TIP
Exercise Is Crucial

The Malinois was bred to work all day, and your dog won't be happy sitting around your house waiting for you to come home from work. He needs plenty of vigorous exercise every day. If you work away from home, you might consider taking your Mal to doggy day care so he can play while you work.

To encourage your Belgian Malinois to enter the crate on his own, try tossing a few treats inside. Initially, he'll probably reach in to get the treats and immediately back out. With plenty of practice and positive reinforcement, he should get more and more comfortable stepping inside the crate. As his comfort level increases, you can try shutting the door behind him for a second or two before rewarding him with praise and treats. With practice, you can leave the door shut for longer and longer periods of time. At this stage in your dog's crate training, it's important that you don't let him out if he begins to bark or cry. Releasing him while he's upset will only reward him for such behavior, increasing the likelihood of him repeating the behavior in the future. Instead, give him time to settle down and release him when he's quiet. Soon, he'll begin to understand that the crate is not a place to be feared but a place to rest and relax.

Supplies

When preparing for the arrival of your Belgian Malinois, you need to make a list of essential supplies to make sure you have everything you need before the new dog's arrival. Even if you have other dogs in your home, you may want to make a list anyway. New toys and bedding can help prevent territorial behavior.

Food – One of the most important items on your list will be puppy food. It would be a disaster to bring your Belgian Malinois home only to discover you have nothing to feed him and the pet stores have closed for the evening. Ask your breeder or rescue staff what your new dog is currently eating and pick up a small amount of that type of food. Even if it's not what you intend to feed your dog long-term, it's best to use it for the first few days and switch food slowly to prevent digestive upset. Be sure to ask about any food allergies or sensitivities, so you can make sure to buy diet-appropriate food and treats.

Leash and collar – Another important item is an appropriately sized collar for your new Belgian Malinois. Most styles of collar are adjustable, so if you aren't certain about what size you need you should be able to estimate. Your local pet store or favorite online retailer likely has a vast selection of collars and leashes to choose from. Whether you prefer something delicate and feminine or brightly colored and fun, you should be able to find a collar and leash to match your new dog's personality. When choosing leashes, it's also important that you choose one that's appropriate for your dog's size. Thin leashes may be okay for puppies, but they may not be able to hold up to an adult Malinois lunging after a squirrel on your daily walk. Don't forget to get an identification tag with your phone number or address as well, just in case your new companion manages to escape.

Dog bed – Shopping for dog beds can be an overwhelming task, with so many styles and sizes to choose from. Some can be quite expensive, so you want to make sure your dog will appreciate his new bed. Some dogs enjoy sleeping curled up in a ball, while others prefer to lie flat, so if you know how your dog likes to sleep you can choose accordingly. You also have the option of buying an inexpensive bed now and investing in something nicer later. Whichever style you choose, be sure to buy one with a removable cover for ease of washing. Many Malinois enjoy chewing, so you might also want to look for a bed made of durable material. If you're bringing home an adult Malinois, especially a senior, you might consider purchasing a memory foam bed, which is easier on a dog's aging joints.

Toys – Belgian Malinois are known for their powerful jaws, so you want to look for toys designed for heavy chewers. Regardless of the type of toys you bring home, remember that supervision will be necessary during playtime to ensure that your dog doesn't break pieces off to swallow or choke on.

Grooming supplies – Even if you plan on having a professional groomer care for your Belgian Malinois, you may still want to pick up a few grooming supplies. The more you can accustom your dog to the grooming process at home, the better behaved he'll be for the professionals. Since Malinois have a low-maintenance coat, you won't need many supplies. A simple bristle brush or shedding blade should be enough to help with shedding. Shampoos and conditioners will help keep your dog looking and smelling fresh between visits to the groomer as well. If you plan on trimming your Malinois' nails at home, you will want to invest in a high-quality nail trimmer. If you're feeling overwhelmed by your local pet store's selection of grooming products, you might consider asking a groomer for advice on which tools are best for the breed.

Housetraining supplies – Whether you're bringing home a puppy or an adult Belgian Malinois, you should also include housetraining supplies on your shopping list. Moving into a new household is a stressful event and even the most well-trained dog can have an accident. It's better to be prepared than to realize you have nothing to clean the mess with. Disposable or reusable puppy pads can be useful for dogs of all ages and make cleanup a breeze. There are also many types of cleaning products on the market that contain enzymes and other ingredients to help eliminate pet odor and stains. If you're interested, you may also be able to find special bells to hang on your door so that you can teach your dog to paw or nose them to let you know when he needs to go out. The most important tool in your housetraining toolkit is the crate, so be sure you have one ready so that you can start crate training as soon as you bring your new family member home.

Basic Shopping List for Your New Belgian Malinois

- Collar and leash
- Identification tag
- Crate
- Bedding
- Food
- Food and water bowls
- Treats
- Toys
- Combs or brushes
- Shampoo
- Nail trimmer
- Puppy pads
- Cleaning supplies

Puppy-Proofing Your House

The final step in preparing your home for your Belgian Malinois is to puppy-proof the areas to which your dog will have access. The most helpful method of puppy-proofing is to get down on the ground at your puppy's level to see what he may be able to reach. You'll need to go through your house, room by room, to make sure all potential dangers are either removed or placed out of your puppy's reach. Once you've finished puppy-proofing all indoor spaces, you'll need to move outside and repeat the process in your yard or garden.

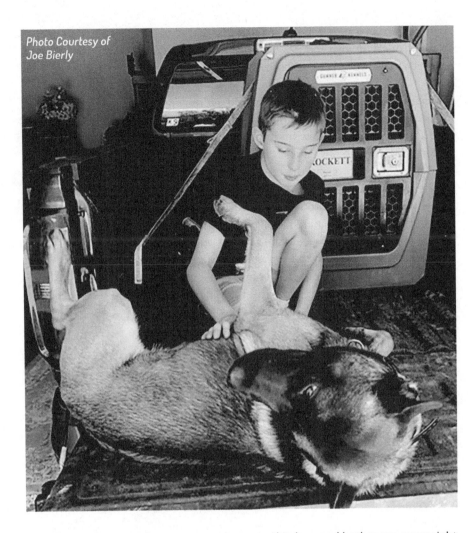

Photo Courtesy of
Joe Bierly

When puppy-proofing rooms such as your kitchen and bathroom, you might consider investing in child-proof locks for your cabinets, especially if your cabinets contain anything that could be harmful to your Malinois such as chemicals or a trashcan. Pick up all electrical cords from the floor and remove anything that is plugged into the wall at a puppy's eye level such as nightlights or air fresheners.

In the living room, you'll need to move items such as TV cables and house-plants to a place high enough that your puppy cannot reach them. Plastic zip ties can be helpful in moving electrical cords out of the way and securing them without any permanent effect on your furniture or décor. If you have particularly valuable furniture or antiques, it might be a good idea to put them away until your puppy is through his teething stages and understands the rules of the household.

Curtains and blinds may also hang low enough for your puppy to get into trouble with. Though you should never leave your puppy outside of his secure area without proper supervision, removing temptation will help your puppy learn more quickly without the frustration of having precious items damaged.

If your puppy will have access to any of your bedrooms, you'll need to make sure that everything is picked up off the floor. This includes laundry, shoes, and children's toys. It can take only a moment for your Malinois to swallow a toy or sock, which can easily cause choking or an intestinal blockage. Again, you'll also need to make sure that all electrical cords and houseplants are placed up and away from your puppy.

Indoor Dangers

One of the most common dangers facing your puppy are electrical cords. Remember, puppies explore their world with their mouth, so their first instinct when confronted with something interesting is to bite it. Rather than deal with the potentially fatal consequences of an accident, it's best to pick up electrical cords or move them out of your puppy's area. Electrical cord covers are also an option, but supervision will be necessary until your puppy understands that the cord covers are not toys.

Cleaning products, pesticides, and other household chemicals also pose a danger to curious puppies, so you'll need to make sure that all chemicals are kept far away from your new dog. Other household dangers include medication, beauty and hygiene products, and plant food and fertilizer. These products should all be kept behind closed doors or on shelves high enough that your dog cannot reach them.

As you go through your house, take note of any houseplants you may have and research their toxicity. Toxic plants can cause a variety of health problems if consumed, ranging from mild gastrointestinal distress to death, so you may need to rearrange your décor to accommodate your puppy's curiosity and either get rid of toxic plants or keep them out of reach. The ASPCA has a complete list of common houseplants that are toxic to dogs on their website. Many types of houseplants are non-toxic to dogs, but you still don't want your dog destroying your beautiful foliage, so make sure he cannot reach them.

Stairs are another potential danger, especially to young puppies or elderly adult dogs. Puppies and seniors have limited physical strength and are often unable to safely navigate long flights of stairs on their own. Serious injuries can occur if they misstep and take a tumble. Pressure-mounted baby gates are a great way to keep your dog safe without causing your human family members too much inconvenience.

Finally, you'll need to make sure that your trashcan is secure and cannot be opened by your new dog. It may not seem like an obvious danger, but trashcans contain everything from broken glass to toxic food and plastic. As this bad habit is self-rewarding, dogs will quickly learn that the trashcan is a source of interesting and tasty treats, so it's best to prevent your dog from developing this behavior in the first place. If you cannot secure your trash inside a cabinet, there are many trashcans on the market designed to lock to keep pets and wild animals out.

Outdoor Dangers

Once you've removed all indoor dangers from your home, it's time to puppy-proof your outdoor spaces. As you did inside your house, you'll need to get down to your puppy's level to search for potential dangers. Most importantly, you'll want to walk along and closely examine every inch of your fence line. Look for holes, loose boards, rotten wood, broken latches, or any other way your dog could escape your yard. The world beyond your yard is a dangerous place full of speeding cars, wild animals, and even humans with bad intentions.

A secure fence will help keep your new family member as safe as possible. Not only is it important that your fence does not contain any holes or weak spots, it's important that it is made of a material that is difficult to climb, such as wood planks. Malinois are known for their athletic ability and are more than capable of climbing a chain-link fence of nearly any height. If you plan on using any type of outdoor dog run, you will need to make sure the top is covered as well to prevent your dog from climbing out.

One of the biggest dangers of your outdoor space is the exposure to the elements. If you plan on leaving your dog outside for any period of time, it's important that you provide him with proper shelter and fresh water at all times. It is not recommended to leave your dog outside without supervision for long periods of time, but if you must do so, you need to make sure that he has enough fresh water and is able to escape the heat of the sun or any snow or rain. It is never acceptable to leave your dog outside during extreme temperatures. Although the coat of the Belgian Malinois will keep his temperature regulated to some extent, heat stroke and frostbite are possible if your dog is exposed to extreme temperatures for long periods of time.

If your home has a pool, make sure the fence surrounding it is secure and that your dog is unable to squeeze between the rails. If your pool does not have a fence, you'll need to make sure that your dog never has unsupervised access to the area. It can take only a moment for a dog to fall in and even the best swimmers can find themselves disoriented and unable to find a way out.

As you did indoors, you'll also need to take note of the plants in your outdoor space and research their toxicity. Toxic plants should be removed or fenced off to prevent your Belgian Malinois from consuming them. Even if your vegetable garden is not considered toxic, you may not want your new dog digging up your vegetables, so you may want to fence that area off. It's not uncommon for dog owners to only allow their dogs access to part of their outdoor space to make room for their other hobbies.

If your outdoor space includes access to your garage or shed, you'll need to make sure that all antifreeze, pesticides, and other harmful chemicals are kept behind closed doors on shelves out of reach of your new companion. Antifreeze poisoning is an especially common, yet preventable accident. Antifreeze has a sweet flavor that pets find appealing, so you'll need to make sure that any leaks are cleaned up and containers are stored away. If consumed, antifreeze causes severe kidney damage and can be fatal. As you go through your home removing toxic items, you may consider looking up the phone number for your local poison control center to place somewhere handy, just in case.

CHAPTER 6

Bringing Your New Belgian Malinois Home

The Importance of Having a Plan

"Any Malinois pup from a reputable breeder will have already begun some type of imprinting by the time the pup arrives in its new home. This will give the new handler a head start with house breaking, crate training, etc. Find out the pups daily routine and use what's already been done to your advantage."

MARK ROTH JR.

BlackJack Malinois

The frantic chaos of bringing a new dog into an unprepared home is overwhelming for a nervous puppy or adult dog. Rather than getting off to a bad start, set your relationship up for success with a plan that covers everything from picking your dog up through his first night in your home.

An important step in developing your plan is discussing the rules of the house with your family. If you have other dogs, this may be easy, as you already have boundaries in place for them. However, if you don't have any other dogs, you'll need to decide what behaviors will be acceptable in your home. For example, where will the new dog sleep? At first, he'll probably need to sleep in a crate or playpen until you're more confident in his housetraining, but in the long run will he be allowed to sleep in bed with his humans or in his own bed on the floor? Will he be allowed on furniture? You might also want to discuss how you expect your dog to greet visitors. Some owners allow their dogs to politely sniff new people, but never jump on them, while others may prefer that their dog watches politely from his own bed or crate.

Going through your plan with other members of the household is a great way to make sure everyone is on the same page. You may also want to write everything down, especially if you're prone to forgetting things or simply need a visual representation of your plan. Introducing a new family member can be a stressful time, but as long as you develop some sort of plan prior to your new dog's arrival, everything should go smoothly.

Developing a Schedule

Prior to your Belgian Malinois' arrival, you'll want to consider what a normal day will look like for you once your new dog is home. Think about what time you wake up in the morning, when you will serve him breakfast, and when or if your family will need to leave for work or school. A puppy will not be able to go more than a couple hours without a bathroom break, so you'll need to consider how flexible your schedule will need to be in order to accommodate his tiny bladder. Think about your usual evening schedule and decide who will need to feed the new dog his dinner.

It can be helpful to write down your family's weekly schedule to help decide who will be responsible for the dog at certain times throughout the day. Although smaller children

Photo Courtesy of
Kaylin Hall

may not be able to be relied upon for much, they can help out with feeding and cleanup. Older children can take on as much responsibility as you think they're ready for. It's helpful to assign each family member certain tasks to make sure everything is done correctly. Without clear communication, the puppy's evening walk could be forgotten, or he could be served multiple breakfasts. Though neither of these situations is going to harm your dog, it's not going to help him adapt to your lifestyle. The more consistent you can be in your schedule, the more quickly he'll understand what is expected of him in his new home.

Picking Your Dog Up from the Breeder or Shelter

If you've done your home-work, you should be completely prepared to bring home your Belgian Malinois from the breeder or shelter. However, it doesn't hurt to double-check. Before you pick up your new companion, go through his designated area one last time to make sure it's thoroughly puppy-proofed and ready for his arrival. You might also want to go through your list of supplies to

FUN FACT
Famous Mals

Thanks to their trainability, Belgian Malinois are great to use in TV shows and movies. The TV crime show Person of Interest features a Malinois named Bear, while the 2015 film Max featured a Mal of the same name returning from service with the US Marine Corps.

make sure you don't need to pick anything up. If you do, it's best to go before you arrive at the shelter or the breeder's home. Stopping on the way home will only add more stress to an already overwhelming day for your puppy. Not to mention, taking an unvaccinated or undervaccinated puppy into a store is a risk you don't need to take. You want to make your puppy's transition into his new home as smooth as possible, so try not to stop anywhere on the way home if you don't have to.

If you've already received a copy of the breeder's contract or the shelter's adoption agreement, be sure to read it thoroughly before you pick up your new dog. This way, if you have any questions or concerns about the content of the document, you can bring it up before you leave with the puppy. Most breeders will require a deposit to hold your puppy until he's old enough to leave his mother, so make sure that this amount is marked as paid in the contract and subtracted from the total purchase price. The contract or adoption agreement is a legally binding document, so it's important that it is accurate, and you agree to it in its entirety. If you haven't already paid the full purchase price or adoption fee but are planning to do so when you pick the dog up, make sure you have enough cash or a check ready to go.

In the days leading up to the big day, think of any last-minute questions you may have about your new family member. Whether your questions are about the dog as an individual or the breed itself, be sure that you're heading home with as much knowledge as you're comfortable with. If you don't have any questions now, don't fret. Most breeders and shelter staff are happy to maintain contact after adoption, so if you think of any questions later, you should be able to ask them when they come up.

The Ride Home

The trip from the shelter or the breeder's home to your house may seem like an insignificant event, but it can be a scary experience for a puppy who has just left his mother and siblings for the first time. It's likely that he has had little to no experience in a car, so he may be nervous. Since this won't be the last time your Belgian Malinois will need to travel in a vehicle, you want to try to make it as positive an experience as possible for him. No matter what happens, it's important that you remain as calm as possible during the drive. The excitement of bringing home a new dog won't help a frightened puppy. He won't understand that your elevated emotions are due to his presence and not the car ride itself. The same concept applies to adult dogs, especially those coming from a shelter. You may not know how much experience the dog has with cars, so it's crucial that you approach the ride home with calmness and confidence.

No matter what age your Belgian Malinois is, you'll need to make sure that he is safely restrained for the duration of the ride home. It can be tempting to have him ride comfortably in your lap, but that is a dangerous option for everyone in the vehicle. There are many different options for restraints, depending on your new dog's experience level and size. Dogs of any age are typically quite comfortable riding in a crate. Not only does the enclosed space of the crate keep them safe, it can give them a sense of comfort, especially if you can give them a blanket or toy with the scent of their mother and littermates. For more experienced dogs, or adults that require a crate too big for the vehicle, a seatbelt is another option. Most doggy seatbelts feature a comfortable harness with a leash-like attachment that usually clips into the seatbelt buckle or wraps around the headrest. If you'd prefer that your Belgian Malinois have access to the entire back seat or cargo area of your car, you might also consider using a metal or fabric barrier to keep him in place. Remember, unrestrained dogs can be a danger to you and other drivers, so make sure that your new family member stays safe and sound until you reach your home.

One of the most common reactions to car rides is motion sickness, especially with dogs that haven't ridden in cars much. However, it's possible that even the most experienced travelers can become carsick, so it's best to prepare for the worst-case scenario just in case. Disposable or reusable puppy pads, towels, or blankets are all great for lining crates or cargo areas to keep your car clean. If you're using a seatbelt or barrier to restrain your dog, you might consider investing in a waterproof seat or cargo area cover. It's also suggested that you bring along a plastic bag or other container for soiled blankets or towels, just in case your new dog does get sick.

Photo Courtesy of
Allison Levey

Some dogs may react badly to their first experience in cars. Some will shake nervously, but remain quiet, while others may panic and try to escape. This is yet another reason that safety restraints are necessary. No matter how your dog reacts to the car ride, remember to stay as calm as possible. Your anxiety will only worsen your dog's panic. Even if you don't feel calm, it's important to give your dog the impression that you have everything under control.

Introducing Your Belgian Malinois to Your Family

One of the most nerve-wracking aspects of bringing a new dog home is the introduction to your family members, both human and animal. This is a crucial time in your new Belgian Malinois' life, so you want to make sure your introductions go smoothly.

If you have other pets in your home, especially dogs, you'll need to introduce your Malinois to your existing pets in an area of your home that might be considered neutral territory. This will include any space where your current pets do not spend much time such as a front yard, formal dining room, or even an infrequently used guest room. You won't want to stray far from the safety of your home if you're bringing home an unvaccinated or undervaccinated puppy as you risk exposing them to potential illnesses.

To ensure everyone's safety, it's best to restrain both your new Belgian Malinois and your current pets and introduce them one at a time. Although you might expect everything to go well, it's important that you can separate them quickly if necessary. A harness and leash are ideal for this as you can pull the pets apart quickly without risking injury to their necks as you would with collars.

Allow the animals to view each other from a distance at first to gauge their comfort levels. If they seem comfortable and excited to meet, you can allow them to get closer or even let them sniff each other. If at any point either dog shows anxious body language, such as a stiffened body, raised hackles, or growling, you'll need to back off and give them each enough space to relax a bit before moving forward.

No matter how comfortable your pets seem with each other, it's important that you do not allow them unsupervised access to each other during the first few weeks or months together. Accidents can happen quickly and it's best to be there so that you can stop any bad behavior before it escalates into a fight. Supervising does not mean you're present in the room but not paying attention. You'll need to actively monitor each animal's body language to make sure neither one is displaying fearful, anxious, or aggressive behavior.

Some dogs may need more time getting to know one another, so if your pets don't seem to get along at first, don't panic. Just go slow and don't rush them. Rushing your pets into a relationship they're not interested in can leave a lasting negative impression on them both. Instead, take your time and allow the animals to take the lead on how comfortable they are with one another.

Introducing your new Belgian Malinois to your children is a bit easier than introducing him to your pets because you can have a conversation with your kids about the do's and don'ts of interacting with a new dog. If you have other dogs in your home, they may already understand the basics of safe interactions, but it can be helpful to reiterate those rules. When the kids see the adorable puppy for the first time, they can get excited and frighten the puppy, so it's important to explain that they need to be calm and gentle with the new pet.

As with other animals, supervision will be necessary any time your new Malinois is interacting with your kids. Especially young children may not understand that the puppy cannot be handled the same way as their toys. A fall from

Photo Courtesy of
Hailey Byrne

the arms of a child may not seem like much, but it's enough to cause serious injury, so it's crucial that you explain that the children are not allowed to pick the puppy up. If they want to hold him, they can sit on the floor and invite him into their laps. Regardless of the age of your new dog, encourage your kids to be as calm and gentle as possible to help make the new family member feel welcome in his new home.

As always, if your children or the new dog shows any signs of nervousness or fear, it's essential that they be separated right away. Too much excitement can also escalate quickly, so you may need to give everyone a break to settle down before resuming play. This is why supervision is so important at this stage. It takes only a moment for things to go wrong, so you want to keep an eye on the situation at all times so nobody gets hurt. You might also want to explain to the children that they are not to interact with the new dog unless there is an adult in the room. Eventually, you'll be able to trust them together, but you'll need to monitor their behavior until you're sure that both children and dogs understand the rules.

The First Night Home

"The first few days/nights will set the tone for the rest of the dog's life. Firm, consistent guidelines need to be set from the very beginning."

SUZANNE J BELGER
Desert Mountain Malinois

It's best if you can bring your new Belgian Malinois home on a weekend or a night where you don't have any early appointments the following morning. It's unlikely that your new dog's first night home with be very restful. Even adult dogs who know the rules of bedtime can be unsettled during their first night in a new home. For puppies, this will be their first night away from their littermates and mother, so it can be an especially stressful experience.

As tempting as it may be to put your Belgian Malinois to bed on the other side of the house and out of earshot, isolation will only result in fear and anxiety. Instead, it's best to keep your new companion as close as possible. While you don't want to allow an unhousetrained dog to sleep in your bed with you, you can set up his crate or playpen next to your bed. As long as he's able to see and smell you, he's going to be far more comfortable than he would be on his own.

This first night will be an opportunity to set up your nightly routine. You'll want to take your new dog outside to relieve himself as late as possible, so try to make it the last thing you do before bedtime. If you've brought home a puppy,

*Photo Courtesy of
Gail Lavelle*

you'll still be up every few hours to take him out, but at least you can get a couple hours of sleep before the next bathroom break. Remember, the rule of thumb is that puppies can hold their bladder and bowels for one hour for every month of their age. So, a four-month-old puppy will need to go outside approximately every four hours. Any longer and you risk a mess.

You can be fairly certain that your new Belgian Malinois is going to cry during the night, but you'll need to determine whether those cries are a demand for attention or a request to go outside. If you've just come in from a bathroom break, you can be fairly certain that the dog's cries are for attention. Although it may be difficult to ignore the whining, barking, and howling, if you respond, your Malinois will learn that barking will get your attention. If you ignore him, he'll eventually realize that it's not getting him anywhere and settle down to sleep. If it's been several hours since his last bathroom break, however, you can be certain that the dog's cries mean that he's ready for a trip outside. Throughout this first night, it can be helpful to note the approximate times that your puppy asks to go outside. The more consistent you can be in the following nights, the more quickly your puppy will understand the routine and the more sleep you'll be able to get.

CHAPTER 7
The First Few Weeks

"Probably the most important thing a new owner will need to prepare for is time. Time is needed for the owner and dog to get to know each other."

RAYMOND FARBER
Farbenholt Kennels

Standing by Your Expectations

The first few weeks of life with your new Belgian Malinois will have its ups and downs, so it's crucial that you are realistic about what to expect from your new family member. It's important to keep your expectations fairly low during this tumultuous time. A new dog, whether it's a puppy or an adult, is a huge commitment and you need to remember that you're only going to see progress in your dog's training if you put the time in. Dedicating a single 30-minute period each week to your Malinois' training is certainly better than nothing at all, but you can't expect the same amount of progress as you would if you were doing shorter, daily sessions. In fact, infrequent training may result in a dog that is uninterested and even resistant to your training. This is because you're going to need to spend time each session going over what you taught in the last session. If you only train once a week, your training sessions are bound to be repetitive, which is unlikely to keep your dog interested and engaged.

Of course, this doesn't mean you need to spend every moment of your day working with your Belgian Malinois either. Remember, this is a new situation for him too, so it will help to be a bit forgiving of his behavior during this time. It's possible that he learned the rules of the house, and maybe even a few commands, in his prior home, but the stress of rehoming can cause him to forget or act out. Rather than dive directly into a full-time training program as soon as you bring your Malinois home, opt for short, fun training sessions each day. Keep it light with plenty of positive reinforcement. At first, these sessions may be as simple as introducing your dog to his new name. Avoid overwhelming your dog during the first few weeks together. If all he learns are the rules of the house and nothing more, consider that a win. Consistency is key in dog training, but low expectations at the beginning will help ensure that your relationship gets started on a positive note.

Establishing Household Rules

"Your Malinois puppy will likely outsmart you, many times. They are exceptionally skilled at teaching their owners how they want them to behave."

JANET WOLFF
Stahlrosenhof Intl K-9

Photo Courtesy of Coco Marin

During the first few weeks with your new Belgian Malinois, you're going to need to work consistently to establish the rules of the household. It's important to decide on these rules prior to the arrival of your new companion, so that you will know how to handle any problems when they arise. Additionally, each human family member will need to play an active role in establishing the household rules to maintain the consistency needed for your dog to learn.

One of the most important rules to establish with your new dog is that humans should always go through a doorway first. It's rude and inappropriate for dogs to shove their way through a door before a human. Not only does it put the human's safety at risk, as an adult Malinois is big enough to easily knock a person over, but it also puts the dog's safety at risk should he bolt out an open front door. To teach your dog to be polite around doorways, ask him to sit or wait patiently each and every time you open a door. He may get excited at first, especially if the door leads outside. However, he must wait patiently until he is released, so ask him to sit as calmly as possible while you go through the door. Once through, you can invite the dog to come with you, but you must be careful not to allow him to run through until he's given the release command. Soon, he'll begin to understand that he doesn't get to race through doorways whenever a door is opened.

It's also important that you continually remind your Belgian Malinois that he must politely move out of the way when asked. Whether you're asking him to get off the sofa or just move out of your way in the kitchen, he needs to move when

Photo Courtesy of
Kathie Carvajal

he's asked. In a natural pack setting, only the leader of the pack is allowed to stay where he is while the rest of the pack goes around him. Allowing your dog to stay where he is when he's in the way will only enforce the idea that he's in charge.

There are several ways that you can teach your dog to move when asked. The first is keeping a "drag line" on him. A drag line is simply a short leash that he can wear around the house. It's not long enough to get him tangled up on anything, but it's enough that you can grab it if you need to control him. Drag lines can be especially helpful if your dog reacts negatively to his collar being grabbed. Some dogs will nip or bite when their collars are grabbed, so using a drag line will allow you to enforce the rules while keeping your hands away from your dog's teeth.

You can also try luring your dog out of the way with treats. Be sure to do so while giving your command of choice to positively reinforce this behavior. Finally, you can try pushing your dog with your hand, but you risk a negative reaction similar to grabbing him by the collar. Although you're free to use the training method of your choice, using a drag leash along with positive reinforcement will likely get the best results with your Belgian Malinois.

Preparing for Mealtime

Mealtime is an opportunity to teach your new Belgian Malinois respect. It's a time to introduce your dog to the concept of patience and calmness. Your dog should always be willing to sit quietly and wait for his dinner to be delivered. No dog should be allowed to jump around, dive into the food bowl, or knock it out of your hands before you set in on the floor.

Initially, it may take some time for your dog to learn to wait calmly for his meals, especially if he's unfamiliar with the concepts of sitting and staying. If you need assistance in teaching your Malinois these commands, please consult Chapter 12. Basically, you want to ask your dog to sit and wait while you set his food on the ground. Your dog should not immediately dive in the moment the bowl touches the ground. Instead, he needs to wait patiently until you give him an appropriate command to release him. Many owners simply use the word 'okay' to let their dogs know they're free to eat.

If you have children that are old enough to handle this chore, you can teach them how to make the dog wait for his dinner. This is an excellent way of reinforcing to the dog that all human family members are to be respected. It may not seem like a big deal to let your dog eat when he wants to, but this self-control will be the basis for many household rules, such as waiting patiently to walk through an open door rather than bolting out as soon as it's opened. It will also help solidify other commands as you can ask your dog to wait in a sit, stand, or down position.

Playtime with Your Belgian Malinois

It's essential that you always supervise your new Belgian Malinois' playtime. Whether he's playing with children, other pets, or alone with a new toy, you need to monitor him carefully. Without proper supervision, playtime can quickly escalate into a negative experience or even a dangerous situation.

If your new companion is playing alone with toys, he should always be supervised to make sure he isn't destroying the toy. Depending on the type of toy you've given him, it may be possible for him to chew off a piece and swallow it. If he's able to swallow the pieces, he is at risk of choking or developing an intestinal blockage. Both of these situations are costly medical emergencies that can be easily avoided with proper supervision.

If your Malinois is playing with your children or other pets, you must keep a close eye on them to make sure no one is getting overwhelmed or playing too rough. It's crucial to carefully watch everyone's body language and interrupt if things are getting out of control. Playtime should never be too rough as someone can easily get hurt. With dogs, rough play can quickly escalate into a fight if one dog gets hurt or feels threatened by the other dog's aggressive play. You can teach your children how to discourage rough play by imitating the way puppies play with each other. If the puppy nips them, have them yelp and immediately stop playing. At first, the puppy may be confused, but eventually he will understand that playing too roughly will result in the end of the game.

Puppy Problems

"I always tell all of my customers that a Malinois will find something to do if they are not exercised or grow up without structure. That means they will chew up anything. However, as long as training starts early and boundaries are set consistently, new owners will have no problems."

BIRGIT HALL
Chien Policier

While your Belgian Malinois adapts to life in his new home, you're bound to run into a few problems. Most puppy problems are easily corrected, but you'll need to do so consistently in order to prevent your dog from developing bad habits. Preventing bad behavior is always much easier than fixing it later, so you'll want to make sure you're as consistent as possible in your corrections. Part of this consistency is proper supervision and puppy management. Since many bad habits are self-rewarding, you can't allow your puppy to get into a situation where he's able to get away with naughty behavior.

Photo Courtesy of Jacalyn Honeywell

One of the biggest challenges you'll face as a new puppy owner is chewing. Puppies explore the world around them using their mouths, so chewing is a habit that comes naturally to them. This habit intensifies between the ages of four and six months, when puppies are teething. The process of adult teeth replacing puppy teeth can be quite uncomfortable and puppies will resort to chewing in an attempt to soothe their aching mouth. It's crucial that you manage your Belgian Malinois' environment during this time and do not allow him the opportunity to chew on anything inappropriate. Leaving your puppy unsupervised in your house is just asking for trouble, so be sure to place him in a crate or secure area if you are unable to keep an eye on him. To further discourage your puppy from chewing on your furniture or other personal items, try to offer him safe alternatives such as edible chews or toys.

Digging is also a common problem with puppies, so be prepared to closely supervise your Belgian Malinois any time he is enjoying your outdoor space. Turning your dog loose in your backyard and ignoring him is a sure way to encourage him to develop bad habits like digging. Not only is digging destructive, it can also be dangerous. Dogs who dig can easily damage their nails and paw pads. They may also ingest dirt, rocks, or sticks that they dig up. It's also possible that your puppy will be able to dig his way under your fence, allowing him to escape. To prevent any accidents or injuries, it's crucial that you discourage digging from the beginning. It's much harder to correct this behavior once it's established than it is to prevent it from developing in the first place.

Another common puppy problem is excessive barking. Belgian Malinois can be quite vocal, so it's important that you teach your puppy that one or two barks is okay, but any more than that is unnecessary. Allowing your dog to give a warning bark will allow him to fulfill his duties as the protector of the family, but it won't be enough to annoy your family or your neighbors. Many dogs develop this bad habit due to a lack of physical and mental stimulation. As with digging, dogs may resort to barking as a way of entertaining themselves or making their presence known when they're left to their own devices. To discourage excessive barking, you must manage your dog's environment and never give him the opportunity to develop this habit. Barking may also be a problem you encounter when crate training. In crate training, it's essential that you do not release your dog from the crate if he is making a fuss. Once he learns that he will only be released when he is calm and quiet, he'll realize that there's no sense in barking since it won't get him what he wants anyway.

With both excessive barking and digging, you can discourage the behaviors by distracting your dog with a loud noise. A sharp "No!", clap, or stomp is often enough to distract your dog and focus his attention on you instead of the bad behavior. With consistency, your dog will learn that these behaviors will only result in unpleasant noises and he will be unlikely to repeat them in the future. If your dog seems particularly resistant to your corrections, you can try using a water bottle to help discourage bad habits. As you give him a verbal correction, such as "no," you can spray him in the face with the water. Water is completely harmless, but most dogs will not enjoy getting sprayed in the face, so it works quite well to discourage inappropriate behaviors. Never hit, kick, or yell at your dog as a correction. You won't solve the problem and will likely only frighten your dog. Most of the time, puppy problems can be discouraged using minimal corrections, so this type of correction is never necessary or helpful.

Leaving Your Dog Home Alone

The first few times you leave your Belgian Malinois home alone can be stressful for both you and the dog. With a little preparation, the stress can be minimized, which will discourage your dog from developing separation anxiety. Separation anxiety can be incredibly difficult to fix, so it's best to prevent it.

When leaving your home, or arriving home, you must remember not to make a big deal out of it. It can be hard to not give your dog a loving goodbye or a warm greeting after a long day at work, but you must resist this urge. Instead, ignore your dog's excitement or anxiety. Eventually, he'll calm down and you can give him attention then. You want to discourage your dog from experiencing elevated emotions surrounding your arrival or departure. If he gets too excited or stressed out, he'll begin to anticipate these moments and develop separation anxiety. By not feeding into his excitement, you're letting him know that everything is fine regardless of whether you're home or not. The calmer you are in these situations, the calmer your dog is likely to be.

It can be difficult to introduce this concept if you only leave your house for long periods of time, such as going to work. To give your dog the confidence that you'll be back soon, and he doesn't need to worry, try leaving the house for just a few seconds or minutes at a time. You can grab your keys, put on your jacket, and do everything as you normally would, except that you'll only stay outside for a moment. With repetition, your Malinois will begin to be less concerned when you start going through the motions of getting ready to leave. With practice, you can begin increasing the amount of time you leave for. You can take a walk around the block, check the mail, or run errands, and not worry that your dog is stressed about your absence.

It's also important to note that dogs are pack animals, and many will do better with a companion. If your Belgian Malinois is your only dog, you may want to consider adopting another pet to keep him company while you're away. Some dogs will prefer the companionship of their own kind, but many dogs will do well with other species, such as cats. It's important to take your dog's own individual personality and preferences into account when deciding what type of companion would be best.

Training and Puppy Classes

During your first few weeks with your Belgian Malinois, you may want to consider signing up for puppy classes. Puppy classes are just basic obedience classes intended to teach young dogs basic manners and commands. If you're relatively inexperienced with training dogs, working with a professional may be the best way to meet your training goals and improve your relationship with your dog. Not only will your dog learn skills such as loose leash walking, sit, down, and stay, but your dog will also have the opportunity to be socialized with new people, places, and dogs.

Most puppy classes will require your Malinois to be a certain age before attending class. This is not because your puppy is incapable of learning at a young age, it's simply to ensure that he's old enough to have received the necessary vaccinations to keep him and the other dogs in the class safe. Puppies do not typically have strong immune systems at a young age and parasites and disease can spread quickly. The facility or trainer may also ask for proof of vaccinations and flea and tick prevention before your first day of class.

If you've brought home an adult dog, you won't be able to

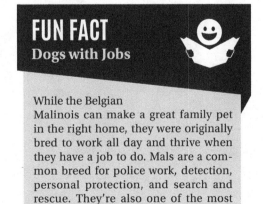

FUN FACT
Dogs with Jobs

While the Belgian Malinois can make a great family pet in the right home, they were originally bred to work all day and thrive when they have a job to do. Mals are a common breed for police work, detection, personal protection, and search and rescue. They're also one of the most common breeds used by the military.

Photo Courtesy of
Janine Blanks

attend puppy classes, but you should be able to find classes appropriate for your dog's age and training level. Depending on where you live, you should have plenty of choices for training classes. From formal obedience schools to individual trainers, you may need to research your options to decide which is best. Some communities also have low-cost training classes to provide help for people on a budget. These classes often donate a portion of their proceeds to local shelters or rescues. You may also choose to have a trainer give you and your dog private lessons at your home or a training facility or park. Private lessons are a great choice for adult dogs who may have socialization issues, or if you're dealing with any behavioral problems. Group classes are ideal for dogs who need a bit of socialization but are not aggressive or overly reactive. Remember, private lessons will likely cost more than group lessons, so it's important to consider not only your budget but what option is best for you and your dog.

Take It Slow

"Ease into it. A tired puppy is a happy puppy! Mal pups can do extraordinary things even at a young age. Remember, words mean nothing to a dog at first and then they mean everything. It is up to us, the handlers to give those words their meaning."

ANTHONY RICHLING
Liberty Dog Camp or Liberty K9

The first few weeks with your Belgian Malinois are likely to have quite a few ups and downs, but it's important to remain patient no matter what happens. There may be times when you feel frustrated and overwhelmed, but there will also be times when you are proud and overjoyed. Remember to keep your expectations low and be patient. Bringing a new dog into your home can be a stressful experience for both your family and your new dog, so just take it slow.

You may want to dive right into training your new Belgian Malinois, but remember, this is a big change for him too. You don't want to stress him out and cause him to dislike training sessions. Try to keep any training sessions you have short and easy. Keep your expectations low and always end on a positive note. If your dog seems to be struggling with a concept, go back to something he knows so that you can reward him for doing something right. You can always come back to the challenge at a later time. The more positive reinforcement you implement in your training, the more your dog will enjoy your sessions together

CHAPTER 8
Health and Wellness

"The keys to keeping a Belgian Malinois healthy and fit are good food, exercise and lots of love!"

BETH ROOD
Roodhaus Belgian Malinois

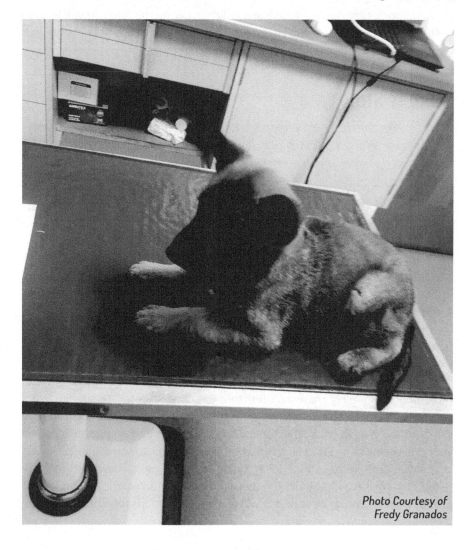

Choosing a Veterinarian

U nless you have other pets in your home and already have an established relationship with a local veterinarian, choosing the right vet for your new Belgian Malinois can seem like a daunting task. However, there are many ways to find a reputable veterinarian to help you keep your new companion as healthy as possible throughout his lifetime.

If you've purchased your Malinois from a local breeder or rescue organization, try asking them for a recommendation. Both breeders and rescues will have ongoing relationships with veterinarians, so they may be able to tell you who they use and trust. Another benefit of using your breeder's preferred vet is that they will have known your puppy since his first visit with his littermates. If you've adopted your new dog from a shelter, rather than a rescue organization, this may be a bit more difficult as many shelters have on-site vets or volunteers.

Unfortunately, if you've adopted your Belgian Malinois from an out-of-state breeder or rescue, you won't have the option of using their preferred veterinarian. Instead, try asking the dog lovers in your life for a recommendation. If you have friends or family with dogs, they may be able to help point you in the right direction. If you attend local dog shows or training classes, you might also ask other participants about where they take their dogs for veterinary care.

Before you begin your search for a veterinarian, you should consider what type of clinic you would like to care for your Belgian Malinois. The vast majority of veterinary clinics offer more traditional veterinary medicine, so if you're interested in holistic or alternative care, you'll need to do some research. The American Holistic Veterinary Medical Association (AHVMA) offers a directory of veterinarians on their website that can be searched by species and treatment type. The American Veterinary Medical Association (AVMA) also has a directory of traditional veterinary practices on their website. You should also consider your schedule when searching for a vet. For example, if you would prefer to take your dog for routine care on Saturdays, then you'll need to find a clinic that can accommodate you. There may even be 24-hour clinics in your area that are available for both routine and emergency care. If you have budgetary limitations, you should also search for low-cost options, as many areas offer vaccinations as well as spaying and neutering at reduced prices for low-income households.

What to Expect During the First Visit

When you bring your Belgian Malinois to the vet for his first visit, he will need to undergo a physical exam before receiving any vaccinations, deworming, or additional testing. To start, he will be weighed, and his heart rate, temperature, and respirations will be measured. Then, the veterinarian will examine him from teeth to tail to ensure that he's healthy. If you have adopted a puppy, it's likely that he will need vaccines during this first visit. Depending on where you've adopted your adult Malinois from, he may or may not need vaccines during his first vet visit. The clinic will likely ask you for a record of your dog's previous vaccines so that they can enter it into their system and provide you with reminders when your dog is due for his next shot.

Photo Courtesy of
Caitlyn Lawing

Around the age of 16 weeks, your Belgian Malinois will be old enough to receive his last round of vaccinations. Prior to this age, it's important that you limit your puppy's exposure to the outside world. Puppies have rather delicate immune systems before they're fully vaccinated, and they can easily contract serious illnesses if exposed. Try to avoid public places and limit the number of strange people and pets that come into contact with your dog. If you notice any symptoms of illness, such as anorexia, weight loss, bloody diarrhea, fever, weakness, or incoordination you need to seek veterinary care as soon as possible. Infections like parvovirus and distemper can be fatal without immediate treatment.

At his first vet visit, your Malinois may also undergo testing for internal parasites. To test for internal parasites, your vet may collect a fecal sample to examine under the microscope, during which a veterinarian or veterinary technician will be able to see any eggs, worms, or protozoa present in the fecal sample. This test is important in prescribing the right treatment, as treatments will vary according to what parasites are present in your dog's stool. Typically, treatments are quite simple and usually involve a few doses of medication, either orally or by injection.

Your vet may also draw a small blood sample to test for heartworm, which is a potentially deadly disease spread by mosquitos. The mosquitos spread the heartworm parasite by feeding on an infected animal followed by biting an uninfected animal. If infected, your dog may need to undergo several months of limited physical activity and medication. Thankfully, with proper treatment most dogs go on to live happy and healthy lives.

If your Belgian Malinois has not yet been spayed or neutered, which is likely if you've adopted a puppy, this is a great opportunity to discuss this with your vet. Most vets recommend spaying or neutering around five or six months of age, but if your dog has any underlying health conditions, it may affect this timeline. Some owners choose to wait until their dogs are closer to nine or twelve months of age before spaying or neutering to allow them to get closer to physical maturity before altering their hormones. Your veterinarian will be able to give you a more accurate timeframe based on your dog's condition. There are also a rising number of owners opting for spaying and neutering alternatives. Vasectomies and ovary-sparing spays are becoming popular among owners seeking more natural methods of caring for their pets. This may not be the right choice for every dog, so it's important to discuss your options with your veterinary team. If costs are a concern, it's helpful to get an estimate for the procedure so that you can save accordingly. Though most dogs undergo anesthesia with few problems, if you have any concerns, now may be a great time to mention them to your vet.

Caring for Working Breeds

While much of the veterinary care provided to working dogs is the same as the care provided to pets, there are a few key differences. With pets, the goal is to simply keep them healthy. With working dogs, care is provided so that the dog can safely perform his working duties. As a canine athlete, a working dog is at a higher risk for injury if his care isn't carefully managed. Physical examinations of working dogs may go beyond the typical hands-on evaluation of a pet. A vet may also analyze a working dog's fitness level, gait, and musculoskeletal structure. Any abnormalities or concerns will need to be closely monitored.

Owners of working dogs will need to keep a closer eye on their dogs for signs of weakness, lameness, or change in performance. It's important to notify your veterinarian as soon as possible so that potential problems can be treated before they seriously affect the dog's performance or career.

Should a working dog become injured, his rehabilitation will need to be carefully managed. High-drive dogs are prone to reinjury simply because they do not enjoy kennel rest and would instead prefer to get back to their normal activity levels. Depending on the area you live in, you may be able to find a vet that specializes in canine rehabilitation and reconditioning to help your dog recover.

Nutrition is also an important focus of caring for a working canine. A knowledgeable veterinarian or certified canine nutritionist will be able to design a diet that is individualized for your dog's unique needs. Even if they are in the same training program, it's unlikely that two dogs will have the exact same caloric and nutritional needs, so it's important to provide your dog with the right amount and type of energy so that he can perform to the best of his abilities.

FUN FACT
Dog Sport Champions

Thanks to their intelligence, energy, and willingness to work, Belgian Malinois excel at nearly any dog sport they try. They're exceptional at heelwork, agility, obedience, flyball, herding, Schutzhund, dock diving, rally, lure coursing, and field trials—just to name a few!

Providing optimal care for the working dog may require a team effort, rather than relying on the expertise of a single veterinary professional. Depending on where you live, you may be able to find a clinic that can provide everything that your Belgian Malinois needs to reach his potential as an athlete, but you may also need to consider asking several professionals to work together as a team to maintain your working dog's health.

Dangerous Foods

There are many types of human food that are well-known among dog owners as dangerous or toxic foods. Chocolate, alcohol, and caffeine are commonly known as foods that should not be fed to your dog, but there are other types of lesser-known foods that can cause serious health problems as well. Many types of sugar-free candy and gum now contain an ingredient called xylitol that can be lethal in certain amounts if ingested by your dog. Garlic, grapes, and onions are also toxic to dogs. If you suspect that your Belgian Malinois may have eaten something toxic, it's important to contact your vet or local poison control center as soon as possible. The sooner your dog can receive treatment, the more likely he is to survive.

There are also plenty of human foods that are not toxic to dogs, but should only be fed in moderation, if at all. High-fat foods like peanut butter and cheese should be given sparingly. Too much fat in your dog's diet can put unnecessary stress on your Malinois' endocrine system, potentially leading to pancreatitis. Salty foods like popcorn, bacon, and ham should also be limited or avoided. Foods containing lactose, such as ice cream, milk, yogurt, or cottage cheese can also cause digestive upset in some dogs. You should also avoid sugary foods like cookies and candy as these can cause serious digestive problems and over time can contribute to your dog's expanding waistline.

Common Health Problems in Puppies

One of the most common problems found in puppies is internal parasites. Puppies are infected by worms in the womb, through their mother's milk, or by consuming contaminated food, water, soil, or fecal matter. The most frequently found parasites in puppies are roundworms, tapeworms, hookworms, and whipworms. Heartworms, which are found in the bloodstream, are also common in certain areas. Protozoa, such as giardia and coccidia, are also common in puppies of all ages.

If your puppy is infected with internal parasites, you may notice symptoms such as vomiting, diarrhea, anemia, and weight loss. Some puppies may also display a distended stomach and otherwise malnourished body. Lethargy and coughing are also common symptoms. It's also possible that your puppy could be infected and display no symptoms at all. Even if your puppy seems healthy, it may be worthwhile to test him for internal parasites. This way, your veterinarian can prescribe the correct treatment before the parasites begin to have any serious effect on your puppy's health.

External parasites such as fleas and ticks are also frequently found on puppies. External parasites can be picked up from the mother dog, other pets in the home, or any outdoor space. The most obvious symptoms are severe itching, skin inflammation, and hair loss. Some dogs may also develop flea allergy dermatitis, which is an inflammatory reaction to the flea's saliva by your dog's immune system. Fleas and ticks are also capable of carrying Lyme disease, tapeworms, bartonellosis, Rocky Mountain spotted fever, babesiosis, and ehrlichiosis. Heavy flea and tick infestations may also cause severe anemia and lethargy. Since external parasites can be passed to other pets in the home and even people, it's important to treat the problem right away. Many diseases carried by ticks are zoonotic, which means they can be passed from animal to human. Some areas may carry a higher risk of certain infections, so talk to your veterinarian about the right flea and tick prevention routine for your dog.

At some point, it's likely that your puppy will experience gastrointestinal upset. Puppies explore their environment with their mouths and commonly eat things they're not supposed to. Additionally, any sudden changes in diet or stress can also wreak havoc on your puppy's delicate digestive system. Vomiting and diarrhea are common, but rarely life threatening. Most puppies will get over it within a day or two, but if goes on longer than that, or you find blood in your puppy's stool, please seek veterinary care as soon as possible. Bloody stool is a symptom of the deadly parvovirus, so call your veterinarian as soon as possible if you notice this. To prevent general digestive upset, it's important to switch your puppy's food slowly over the period of several days or a week. Treats and edible chews should also be given in moderation. Human food is another common reason for stomach issues in puppies, so limit or avoid human snacks if possible.

CHAPTER 9
Housetraining

Different Options for Housetraining

As a dog owner, you have the choice of using a variety of different housetraining methods and tools with your Belgian Malinois. However, most owners of breeds as big as a Malinois opt for the traditional approach. Traditional housetraining involves teaching your dog that he is only allowed to relieve himself outside. Many owners even choose to teach their dogs to use a certain area of their yard, rather than the entire outdoor space. With practice, you'll be able to teach your Malinois to let you know when he needs a bathroom break. He may alert you by whining, pacing, or pawing at the door. You may also consider hanging bells on your door, which are specifically designed to aid in housetraining.

If you live in a climate with extreme weather, you may also consider training your Belgian Malinois to use puppy pads or indoor potty patches. However, this method is more practical with smaller breeds. One benefit of using disposable or reusable puppy pads or potty patches is that your dog will be able to relieve himself if you're away from home or otherwise unavailable to take him out when he needs to go. Although this option is not popular with adult Malinois, it may be useful as a transitionary tool to help your puppy with housetraining while minimizing any messes in your home.

Giving your puppy the option of using puppy pads is a great way to help keep your house and your puppy's designated area cleaner. Your local pet store or favorite online retailer likely has options for both disposable and reusable pads. Disposable pads are inexpensive plastic pads, not unlike diapers, that can be tossed in the trash after being used. They come in a variety of sizes to suit your space and needs. Unfortunately, disposable pads are quite wasteful, so many environmentally conscious pet owners are now opting for reusable puppy pads. Reusable pads are typically made of several layers of fabric with a waterproof bottom layer. Once soiled, they can simply be washed like any other type of laundry. If the pad is particularly dirty, it can also be hosed off outside prior to being placed in your washing machine.

Indoor potty patches are another option to consider using with your puppy. They can be particularly useful with puppies who have a habit of chewing up or destroying puppy pads. Potty patches are typically made of plastic and feature a patch of fake grass or turf. Urine will drain through the "grass" into the base, which can be emptied as needed. If the patch develops an odor, it can be hosed out and cleaned with a pet-safe disinfectant.

The First Few Weeks

The early stages of housetraining are considered the most challenging part of housetraining any dog. Not only will your Belgian Malinois be getting used to life in a new home, but he'll be learning this new skill while developing the bladder strength to wait for longer periods of time between breaks. To make the most out of the first few weeks of housetraining, you need to remember that patience and consistency are key. Accidents are guaranteed, so you need to be ready to deal with them when they happen.

A common misconception with housetraining is that if your puppy has an accident you should rub his nose in it. This "punishment" will not improve your puppy's understanding of the rules of the house and may even confuse him, which will lengthen the period of time it takes for him to be completely housetrained. Belgian Malinois are incredibly sensitive and this type of punishment can be very upsetting for them. If you find that your puppy has had an accident and you were not able to catch him in the act, the only thing you can do is clean up the mess. Puppies live only in the moment and do not understand punishments for past actions, so just clean up the mess and move on.

Photo Courtesy of Lucinde Perdok

If you do catch your Malinois in the act of relieving himself in your house, it's important to correct his behavior properly. Never hit, spank, or yell at your dog. Overreactions to his behavior will only scare him and he may learn to relieve himself indoors only when you're not looking. Instead, you want to interrupt him with a loud clap or a sharp "No!" and take him outside right away. Once you have him outside, you can encourage the dog to finish by using a command such as "Go potty!" Afterwards, be sure to reward him with plenty of praise and attention. You can even use treats but be sure that he's not so focused on the food that he forgets what he's supposed to be doing.

Photo Courtesy of Sam Sciolino

The Importance of Consistency

"Please be sure to keep to a schedule! After eating, sleeping and playing, most puppies will need to go outside to relieve themselves. The same is true if the puppy is sniffing around or wanders off. Housebreaking will be a breeze if you are diligent with the puppy's schedule."

SUSIE WILLIAMSON
Merson Belgian Malinois

The single most important aspect of successful housetraining is consistency. The more consistently you can reinforce the rules of the house, the quicker your Malinois will learn. To be consistent, you'll need to constantly manage your puppy's environment and never allow him the chance to make a mistake. If your puppy does have an accident, it's likely due to poor management, rather than just bad behavior. To properly manage your puppy during the first few weeks and months of housetraining, you'll need to be sure that he does not have unsupervised access to your home at any time. No supervision is sure to result in messes, so if you aren't able to keep an eye on your puppy it's best to put him in his crate or playpen. It's important for all members of the household to be aware of the puppy's bathroom schedule to help maintain the consistency needed for success.

Once your Belgian Malinois is able to go longer periods of time between breaks, and begins to understand where he should relieve himself, you can relax the rules a bit, but you'll need to be particularly strict until then. Both puppies and adult dogs that have not been housetrained will only be able to go a couple hours between trips outside, so plan on taking your new dog outside frequently. Always take your dog outside after any meals, naps, or play sessions. Remember, consistency and patience are essential during this time!

If you're unsure of how long your puppy should be able to go between potty breaks, a good rule of thumb is that he will be able to wait for approximately one hour for every month of his age. For example, if your Malinois is four months old he should be able to hold it for up to four hours at a time. Any longer, and you can almost guarantee an accident. This rule applies around the clock, so you'll need to take your puppy outside at night as well. Unfortunately, the first few months with a new puppy will require more than a few sleepless nights, but as you get to know your puppy and he begins understanding the rules, you'll be better able to predict when he'll need to go outside.

Positive Reinforcement

Another key aspect in successful housetraining is positive reinforcement. This popular training technique involves rewarding your Belgian Malinois any time he performs a desired behavior, such as relieving himself outdoors. Regular repetition will encourage your dog to repeat the behavior in the future, once he understands what behavior elicits the reward. The higher value the reward, the more likely your dog will be to do what you ask.

As with any other type of training, consistency is crucial. Initially, your puppy will not understand why you're giving him a tasty treat, so you'll need to develop the association between the desired behavior and the reward. It can be easy for a puppy to associate going outside with exploration and play, so you'll need to set clear expectations. The first few minutes of every trip outside must be dedicated to relieving himself, and once that is finished, he can be rewarded with treats, affection, and playtime. No matter how excited your puppy is when you take him outside, you must remain calm and serious until he's gone to the bathroom. You might consider using a verbal command to encourage him to relieve himself. With time, he will associate the command with the correct behavior.

It's also important to time your rewards correctly, or you risk interrupting your dog. If interrupted, he may get wrapped up in the reward and choose to finish relieving himself after going back inside. You want to mark the dog's good behavior with a verbal cue, such as calm and quiet praise, but if he's easily excited you may not be able to reward him at all until he's finished. Once you're sure that he's finished you can lavish him with excited praise, playtime and treats. Remember, it's okay to make a big deal out of this. The more excited you are, the more of a reward your praise will be.

HELPFUL TIP
Crate Training

Even if you don't intend to keep your dog in a crate as an adult, you should use a crate to help with house-training your puppy. Your Malinois is likely to encounter a kennel or crate at some point in his life, so you should take the time to teach him that it's a safe, happy place rather than something to fear.

You may need to get to know your puppy a bit before deciding what type of reward works best for him. Some dogs perform better for food rewards, while others prefer attention or even playtime. Excited verbal praise and petting are the most common choice, unless you remember to grab a bag of treats on your way out the door. Some puppies may also respond well to a game of chase or tug with their favorite toy. Whatever makes your Belgian Malinois happy is what you should use to reward him. If he's allowed to explore the yard on or off leash, you can also reward him with a bit of free time after he's gone to the bathroom.

Cleaning Up

No matter how consistent you are in housetraining, it's guaranteed that you'll need to clean up a few messes. Using the right type of cleaning products with the right techniques will ensure that your home stays clean and sanitary, while discouraging your Belgian Malinois from returning to that same area time and again.

In order to purchase the right type of cleaning product, you'll need to consider what type of floors you have in your house. If you have a variety of floor surfaces, such as both carpet and tile, you might need to buy more than one type of cleaner. Choosing the right type of cleaner will help ensure that your floors stay sanitary and free from staining. Feces can leave dangerous bacteria, and sometimes parasites, on your floors, so it's crucial that you use the right type of cleaning product. In addition to eliminating harmful contaminants, odor control is also vital. Even if you can't smell the stain, your dog may be able to, so consider using cleaners containing enzymes designed to break down odor-causing particles. This will help keep your home smelling fresh and discourage your puppy, or any other pet, from feeling the need to mark the area again.

In addition to cleaning products, you'll also need to prepare a stock of towels, paper towels, and scrub brushes. Paper towels are convenient for cleaning up and disposing of messes but may fall apart if used for scrubbing. Small towels or cleaning cloths tend to be more durable and can be washed after use, rather than being tossed in the trash. If messes occur on hard surface floors, like linoleum or tile, you may want to consider using a scrub brush, especially if the mess happens on the grout between tiles. Household steam cleaners also work well to clean and sanitize your floors, but be sure that your flooring has been sealed appropriately to prevent water damage from the steam.

Obviously, cleaning pet messes out of carpet is going to be more difficult than cleaning hard surfaces such as sealed wood or tile. Be sure to test your cleaning product of choice in an area where any discoloration won't be noticed. You'll also need to be cautious about vigorous scrubbing or the use of brushes, as this may cause your carpet to begin unraveling. If you're dealing with any particularly difficult stains or odors, you may need to consult a professional carpet cleaning service.

Playpens and Doggy Doors

As you become more confident in your Belgian Malinois' housetraining, you may want to consider giving him more freedom than his crate or designated area. A playpen can be a great step up in allowing your puppy more room to roam, while still limiting the opportunities for potential troublemaking. Even if you aren't confident enough to leave your Malinois in a playpen while you're away from home, it can still be a great option if you're home but unable to properly supervise him. He can stretch his legs a bit while you focus on work or household chores. If you like the idea of giving your puppy more space, but still don't trust him completely, consider lining the playpen with puppy pads to help limit the mess. Belgian Malinois can be escape artists, so if you plan on leaving your puppy unattended in his playpen, be sure that he can't climb out or knock over the panels.

If your Belgian Malinois has progressed enough in his training that you can trust him to manage his own bathroom schedule, you might also consider investing in a doggy door. This will allow your dog to take his bathroom breaks when he pleases, rather than waiting for you to take him outside. There are several different types of doggy doors available, so you'll need to decide whether

Photo Courtesy of Eric Stockton

Photo Courtesy of
Ashlee and Rob Redmon

you prefer a temporary installation or something more permanent. Temporary doggy doors can be installed in any sliding glass patio door and are easily removed when they are no longer needed, without any damage to the door or surrounding walls. More permanent options include installing flaps in wooden or metal doors or walls. Most types of doors can be locked, so you can control your dog's access as needed or lock up while you're on vacation. There are also many doors that can only be opened by pets wearing a certain type of tag on their collar. This tag unlocks the door like a key when your dog approaches, but will remain locked to your other pets or any neighborhood strays or wild animals who might try to get in.

It's important to choose the right size door for your dog, so if your Malinois is a puppy, you might consider using a temporary door until he reaches maturity or invest in a door that will be appropriate for his adult size. A door that's too large may have a heavy flap that will be difficult for a small puppy to get through, while a door that's too small will require your dog to squeeze through an uncomfortably small space.

If you do choose to use a doggy door, you'll need to be certain that your outdoor space is completely secure. There can be no open gates, gaps or holes in the fence, or potential dangers. Adult Malinois are capable of climbing over fences six feet or taller, so if your dog has a habit of escaping, you may want to reconsider your use of a doggy door.

CHAPTER 10
Socialization

"All forms of socialization are very important with this breed. I recommend any and all socialization for up and coming Malinois pups. Socialization can be as simple as the dog observing different environments and events without being the center of attention."

MARK ROTH JR.
BlackJack Malinois

The Importance of Good Socialization

The most obvious benefit of properly socializing your Belgian Malinois is that you'll be able to confidently take him nearly anywhere and trust that he'll behave himself. Socialization will give your dog both the confidence and the social skills necessary to handle new people, places, and situations. Whether you're planning on competing with your Malinois or would simply like to take him along to your lunch date at the local café, socialization is an essential part of any training program. However, it's important to remember that as a herding breed, Belgian Malinois can be naturally suspicious of strangers, so socialization will need to be ongoing throughout your dog's life. It isn't something you can do once as a puppy and forget about.

Proper socialization is also crucial in maintaining your Malinois' health and happiness. This is a breed that is devoted to their families, so the more you can include your dog in your daily activities, the happier he'll be. Exploring new places is also a great form of mental stimulation. The more places you can take your dog, the more physical exercise he's likely to get as well, especially if it involves meeting new canine playmates. The more physical and mental stimulation you can provide your Malinois

HELPFUL TIP
Early Socialization Is Key

All dogs need to be introduced to as many people, places, and pets as possible when they are young puppies. This is especially important with the Belgian Malinois, who could react to fear with aggression.

with, the less likely he is to develop destructive habits out of boredom.

Without proper socialization, Belgian Malinois may become aggressive, fearful, or overly excitable. Your dog will become difficult to manage and may even become a liability if he believes he needs to protect his family from new people or dogs. Socialization becomes more challenging as your dog ages, so try to introduce your puppy to as many new situations as possible as soon as he is fully vaccinated. Even if you don't plan on competing with your Malinois, you'll still need to take him on walks as well as trips to the vet or groomer. Proper socialization will help make these events less stressful for both your dog and your family.

Photo Courtesy of David Bunney

Socializing Puppies

"Introduce them to dogs of all sizes starting as a puppy. I do not recommend dog parks at all especially for a puppy. Set up puppy play dates with friends who have friendly dogs or who have puppies close in age to yours."

BETH ROOD
Roodhaus Belgian Malinois

Since most reputable breeders believe that socialization should start as early as possible, your Belgian Malinois may already have a head start on the socialization process when you bring him home. It's important to continue to expose your puppy to new situations as soon as you can, but there is a limit on how much you should expose an unvaccinated or undervaccinated puppy to. Until your puppy is fully vaccinated, you should not risk taking him to any public places or expose him to too many new people or pets. Instead, you can work on socialization at home by exposing the dog to new sights, sounds, and smells. You can also try to expose him to different surfaces such as grass, bare dirt, crinkly tarps, and wooden planks. Make use of the things you have around your home until it's safe to take your puppy out in public.

You should also get your puppy used to being handled so that he's comfortable when it's time to behave for the vet or groomer. The more you can do at home during these early stages, the less work you'll have to do later. During the first few months with your puppy, you're laying the foundation for socialization. Once your puppy is fully vaccinated, you can build on that foundation with the confidence that your puppy understands the basics.

As soon as it's safe to expose your Malinois to more outside experiences, you should begin introducing him to as many new people, animals, and places as possible. If you frequently travel by car and would like your Malinois to accompany you on road trips, now is the time to get him used to it. Try taking him with you while you run errands or visit a friend. Sign up for a puppy class or arrange for doggy playdates if you have friends or family with friendly dogs. If you frequently have guests in your home, begin inviting people over so your Malinois can get used to having strangers in his home without feeling threatened or overwhelmed.

Although it is important to expose your puppy to as many new situations as possible, you should be cautious about frightening or overwhelming him. Socialization will only be successful if your puppy has continuously positive experiences. Even a single negative experience can set him back, so it's important to take things as slow as necessary to maintain his comfort. If your puppy begins to display fearful or nervous body language, you may need to back off. While it's important that your puppy learn to work through his fear, now is not the time to put him into scary situations.

Many dog owners think the dog park is a great place to introduce their puppy to new dogs, but the chaotic atmosphere can be too much for most puppies and may leave your dog with a negative impression of strange dogs. Instead, opt for low-key playdates with just one or two new dogs at a time and make sure that the new dogs are going to be friendly and gentle. It's your responsibility to set your Belgian Malinois up for success, so be sure to manage his environment in a way that will always leave a positive impression.

Socializing Adult Dogs

If you've chosen to adopt an adult Belgian Malinois, it's important that you are aware of the challenges of socializing adult dogs. Adult dogs can be more challenging to socialize simply because you are not aware of their past experiences and the dog may need to overcome past trauma. This can make your adult

Malinois' behavior somewhat unpredictable, so until you get to know your new dog, it's best to start slow and socialize him as if he were an inexperienced puppy. Even if the information given to you by the shelter or breeder suggests that your new dog is well-socialized, it's still best to proceed with caution.

Just as you would if you were working with a puppy, you need to ensure that your adult Malinois is only exposed to situations that will have a positive outcome. This means introducing him only to friendly dogs and just one or two new people or animals at a time. Further details on how to do this are provided in Chapter 11. Taking your dog to a busy park or chaotic area of town in the first few weeks may be more than he can handle, and you may risk him losing trust in you, so take it slow. Start with a quieter park and stay at a distance where your Malinois can watch the action without feeling too excited or overwhelmed. Only proceed when your dog is relaxed and calm.

Patience is an important aspect of socialization, especially with adult dogs. If you're working to overcome past trauma in your dog's life, you'll need to take things slower than usual and be understanding if he gets upset. It can be easy to get frustrated when your new companion struggles in training, but with patience and consistency you'll be able to overcome most challenges. It can take weeks, months, or even years to overcome negative experiences in your dog's past so patience is necessary. If you are having difficulty with socialization or need guidance, don't be afraid to reach out to a professional trainer or canine behaviorist. The sooner you get help, the more quickly you and your dog can get on the right path to socialization.

Lifelong Socialization

As previously mentioned, socialization is not something that should be done during your Belgian Malinois' youth and forgotten about. It will be an important aspect of your dog's training throughout his lifetime. No matter how well you socialize your puppy, if you drop the ball as he grows into adulthood, you may end up with a dog with behavioral problems such as fear or aggression toward strangers. As you work on socialization, you'll be exposing your dog to situations where he might be nervous or frightened. However, with enough positive experiences, your dog will learn to trust you. He'll learn that you won't ever put him into a situation that he can't handle, strengthening the bond between you. This in turn will help other aspects of training as your relationship grows closer.

Additionally, lifelong socialization will be important to your dog's mental and physical wellbeing. The more places you can take him, the more mental and physical stimulation he'll receive in addition to any other training or activities you do.

Not only will your dog enjoy the time spent outside of the house with you, but that time will also provide him with the necessary stimulation to help prevent the development of bad habits or destructive behaviors. A bored Malinois is a destructive Malinois, and socialization is just one aspect of keeping your dog busy and engaged.

Dealing with High Prey Drives

"Please be sure to only socialize your Malinois puppy or adult around other sensible puppies and dogs. Go for walks with friends and their dogs with all dogs on leash. Be mindful of any stress signals and/or domineering behaviors by any of the dogs. You must be your dog's advocate and protector and not all dogs need to be "friends" or like one another, just like not all people want to be friends or hang out with others."

SUSIE WILLIAMSON
Merson Belgian Malinois

Photo Courtesy of Taliet Vielza

Many Belgian Malinois, especially those from working bloodlines, have high prey drives that can make socialization with smaller animals difficult. Herding breeds such as the Malinois often possess a strong instinct to chase animals small enough to be deemed prey, so you should be cautious about introducing your Malinois to new animals off leash. In fact, you may not be able to allow your Malinois off leash until his training has advanced enough that you can trust him not to take off after a squirrel or rabbit. Dogs with high prey drives tend to be so focused on pursuing their prey that they will not hear your recall command, no matter how loud you may be.

Unfortunately, prey drive doesn't manifest only around traditional prey animals such as squirrels. Cats and small dogs can also be at risk. While your Malinois may be perfectly friendly, if he sees an animal that he deems as prey, he may not recognize it as a friend, especially once the smaller creature starts to run from him. If you've brought home a puppy, it's important to begin socializing him to small animals as soon as possible so that you can teach him correct behavior. See Chapter 11 for further details on how to do this. With adult dogs, you'll need to use more caution as they have already developed that chasing behavior. Depending on the strength of your Malinois' prey drive, you may also need to accept the fact that your dog cannot be trusted around small animals. If this is the case, you'll need to manage your dog's environment carefully to avoid putting him in situations where he might hurt another animal.

To discourage your dog from pursuing smaller animals, you'll need to draw your dog's attention away from the other animal and back onto you. Do not yell at your dog or jerk his leash. He's likely to ignore you anyway. You want to encourage him to focus on you rather than punish him for focusing on something else. High value treats are ideal, especially if you work on getting your dog's attention when there are no distractions. Using a verbal command, such as "Look at me!", in addition to the high value treat is one of the best ways of refocusing your dog. Once you have your dog's attention, you can try asking him to perform other commands to keep him focused on you, rather than the other animal. With patience and consistency, you should be able to gain your dog's attention no matter how distracting his environment may be.

Dealing with Fear

"Socialize carefully with dogs that will not be harsh or aggressive with your puppy. Interactions should be managed so that the puppy is not frightened or intimidated."

SUZANNE J BELGER
Desert Mountain Malinois

During socialization, you are guaranteed to encounter situations in which your Belgian Malinois will be afraid. While you don't want to traumatize your new dog, there will be times where he will become nervous or fearful, no matter how carefully you manage his environment. Handling these situations carefully will prevent them from leaving a lasting impression on your dog and teach him to trust you as his handler.

No matter what you're introducing your Malinois to, it's crucial to continuously monitor his body language for signs of nervousness or fear. Mild signs include licking the lips, tucking the tail under the body, trembling, and avoidance. Flattening the ears and yawning are also common signs of anxiety. At this stage of fear, most dogs can be calmed down and kept under control. However, if you do not deal with the situation, your dog's behavior may escalate into panting, pacing, and attempts at escape. If your dog is displaying these behaviors, you need to

remove him from the situation imme-diately as it's unlikely that you'll be able to calm him down. Once panic sets in, it's not uncommon for dogs to react aggressively out of fear, so you need to take your Malinois' early warning signs seriously.

During any experience that frightens your Malinois, your behav-ior may be the only thing preventing your dog from panicking, so you need to monitor your own feelings and behavior as well. If you begin to panic, your dog will understand that there is good reason to be afraid and he will panic too. It's essential that you stay as calm and collected as possible, even if you don't necessar-ily feel that way on the inside. It's also important that you don't coddle or try

Photo Courtesy of Kaitlinn Lewis

to comfort your dog. Again, he may take this as a confirmation that he should be worried. Instead, set an example for your dog by remaining calm and confident. Minimizing your reactions will let your dog know that you're in charge and he has nothing to worry about.

If you do end up in a situation that frightens or overwhelms your Belgian Malinois, it's important that you reflect on the situation to see where things went wrong. Sometimes things happen that you cannot prevent, but often these types of situations are due to a misjudgment in your dog's readiness to handle new experiences. In all aspects of training, your ability to reflect on your own behavior and how it affects your dog is crucial. This is a learning opportunity for you too, so take advantage of the fact that you can learn from a negative experience and handle it differently in the future.

If you recognize that you are not willing or able to handle your dog's fear, you need to contact a professional trainer or behaviorist as soon as possible. Fearful behavior can escalate quickly if not dealt with properly, so it may be best to consult someone more experienced in these types of behavioral problems. If your dog has fear issues, you should also be prepared to spend months or even years working to overcome it. Behavioral problems do not develop overnight, and they do not resolve themselves overnight either. Consistency, patience, and the willingness to ask for help when necessary are key in reaching your goals of overcoming fear.

CHAPTER 11
The Multi-pet Household

Introducing a Puppy to Other Animals

Bringing home a new puppy into a household of existing pets can be stressful. Every pet owner wants the initial introductions to go smoothly so that the relationships between your new family member and your current pets can blossom. Unfortunately, things don't always go as planned, so you need to be thoroughly prepared when the time comes to introduce your Belgian Malinois to your other animals. Typically, when introducing a puppy to other animals, you usually need to worry more about the adult animals' reactions toward the puppy than the puppy's reactions. Most puppies are content to get along with everyone, even if they are a bit nervous or excitable in the beginning.

No matter what species of animal you're introducing your Malinois to, it's crucial that each animal is properly restrained for their protection. While a collar and leash will work fine, a harness is often better as it provides something to grab onto should you need to quickly remove your puppy from the situation. With a collar, if you have to pull your puppy away, you risk hurting his neck. For animals that are difficult to restrain such as poultry or certain livestock, it's best to keep them on the other side of a sturdy fence if possible. This will allow the animals and your puppy to sniff and see each other, while ensuring that no one will get hurt.

When introducing your puppy to other animals, go as slowly as you need to. Let the animals view each other from a distance. If you're doing introductions indoors, use a quiet, less frequently used room to put your pets at ease. If outside, make sure your pets have enough room to step away should they get nervous. Keep a close watch on body language and if either animal begins to display signs of fear, aggression, or anxiety, separate them immediately. In some cases, it might take several sessions to get animals used to each other, so don't get in too much of a hurry.

FUN FACT
Secret Service Pups

The Secret Service uses Belgian Malinois to guard the White House. If you somehow managed to hop the fence, you would be hard-pressed to outrun these athletic dogs!

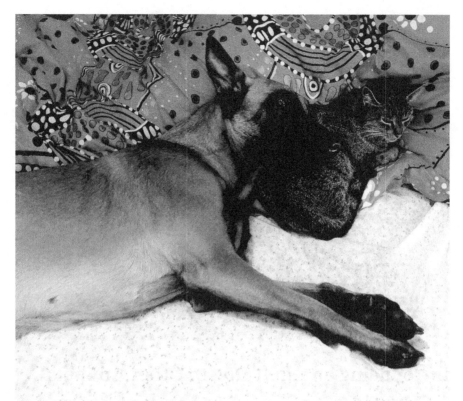

Photo Courtesy of
Sara Golać

During the first few weeks or months with your new Belgian Malinois, it's crucial that you never allow him to interact with your other animals unsupervised until you trust that they can behave themselves. Accidents can happen in the blink of an eye, but they can be easily prevented if you are present and actively monitoring the situation.

As mentioned in Chapter 10, some Belgian Malinois have high prey drives, which can make introducing them to certain types of animals a bit more challenging. Your chances of teaching your Malinois to behave around smaller prey animals are greater when you start introductions at a young age. However, it's important to realize that some Malinois may never be trusted to coexist peacefully around prey animals. Until you know how your new dog is going to react around animals such as rabbits, cats, and chickens, you'll need to use caution during any interaction. With training, all dogs can improve their impulse control, but you might need to accept that unsupervised interactions will never happen.

Introducing an Adult Dog to Other Animals

It's not uncommon for adult dogs to be adopted into new homes with relatively little known about their past experiences. For this reason, introducing an adult dog to other animals in your home can be a bit more challenging than it would be with an inexperienced puppy. Your adult Belgian Malinois may have little to no experience with other pets or livestock, or it may be possible that he had negative experiences. Unless you've adopted your Malinois from a breeder or someone who thoroughly knows the dog's history, it's unlikely that you can be sure of what types of animals he's been introduced to. You should begin introductions as if your new dog has no experience whatsoever but use plenty of caution.

Just as you would when introducing puppies to new animals, you want to make sure that each animal is properly restrained. Adult Malinois are much larger and stronger than puppies, so it's important to make sure that your dog can't pull away from you and injure another animal. Likewise, even a glancing kick from a cow or horse can be enough to seriously injure a dog, so be sure that you are prioritizing everyone's safety. If things go south, make sure you can separate the animals quickly. Once your precautions are in place, you can proceed with the introductions in the same manner as you would with a puppy.

It's important to note that more patience is often required when introducing an adult dog to another animal. Go as slowly as you need to in order to maintain each animal's comfort and safety. You may need to repeat these sessions several times before the animals are comfortable with each other. If you encounter any difficulties with your Malinois' behavior, such as fear or aggression, or you are struggling to control your dog's reactions, seek professional help as soon as possible. A professional trainer or behaviorist will be experienced in this type of behavior and will be able to develop a training plan to correct your dog's behavior so that he can behave more safely around other animals.

Fighting and Bad Behavior

"Malinois are extremely smart, they learn very fast and are the best problem solvers. However, they also know how to get away with bad behavior very fast that is why it is extremely important to be consistent with training."

BIRGIT HALL
Chien Policier

Aggression should never be taken lightly as it can escalate quickly. Dogs do not start out by attacking other animals. Instead, fights typically happen because the warning signs have been ignored. A simple growl or pushing another dog away from a food bowl or toy may not seem like a big deal, but if your Malinois does not face any consequences for his behavior, it is likely to escalate into more dangerous conduct. Fights can result in serious and often life-threatening injuries, especially if the other animal is significantly smaller than your Malinois, so it's important that you address aggression immediately. Never allow your Belgian Malinois to display resource-guarding behavior or bully your other animals. Of course, this doesn't mean your pets aren't allowed to have personal boundaries, but those boundaries should be reasonable. If you witness aggressive behavior, interrupt your dog with a loud clap, stomp, or "No!" Redirecting your dog's behavior by calling him away from the situation or asking him to perform basic commands is often enough to defuse the situation and prevent a fight.

If your Malinois is displaying aggressive behavior, it's crucial that you determine the cause of his aggression. Correcting the behavior is important, of course, but you'll never able to completely solve the problem until you know its source. Take note of every situation where your dog becomes aggressive and look for similarities. If your dog gets upset over sharing his toys, you may need to separate your dogs for playtime or remove the higher value toys from your home.

Resource-guarding behavior can be particularly problematic, so you'll also need to begin working with your dog on how to share. Once you know what triggers your dog's aggression, you can begin working on the problem.

If your dog's aggressive behavior does escalate into an actual fight, you need to use extreme caution when intervening. Do not break up the fight by grabbing one or both dogs with your hands. Most of the time, the dogs are so focused on the fight that they do not care what they're biting, and you could become seriously injured. Depending on how committed your dogs are to the fight, it may be easy to break it up or you may need to resort to more extreme measures. For minor scuffles, loud noises may enough to snap them out of it and end the fight. This is the only situation where yelling at your dogs is appropriate. Stomping, clapping, or banging on your dogs' metal dishes may also work. If it doesn't, try throwing water on the dogs.

Emptying a water bowl or spraying the dogs with a garden hose or spray bottle is typically surprising enough to dogs that they stop fighting. Tossing a

*Photo Courtesy of
Erik Stockton*

blanket or sheet on fighting dogs may also confuse them long enough for you to separate them. If you have no other choice but to physically intervene, first decide which dog is the aggressor. Once decided, grab the more aggressive dog by both hind legs and quickly pull him away from the other dog. You can either pull straight back or swing the dog to the side, but whichever you choose, be sure to do it quickly. If you aren't quick the dog may turn around and bite you. Once the dogs have been pulled apart, restrain or separate them as quickly as possible to prevent them from attacking each other again.

Fighting is a serious behavioral problem that can be difficult to manage. Not only are fights dangerous to the animals in your home, but it's possible for your human family members to get hurt as well. You must be willing to recognize when the situation is out of your control and seek professional help immediately. Aggression is not something that will get better over time and if you are unable to deal with it, you need to get help before a tragedy occurs.

Raising Multiple Puppies from the Same Litter

It can be tempting to consider bringing home two or more Belgian Malinois from the same litter, especially if you have no other pets in your home to keep your new dog company. Littermates will have been together since birth, so they'll be more confident going into new situations together and you won't need to worry about introducing an unfamiliar dog or ever leaving your new companion home alone. Keeping your dog busy will also be less of a problem since he'll always have a playmate available even if you're busy with household chores or away at work.

However, there are plenty of drawbacks to having multiple puppies from the same litter. More puppies mean more trouble and more of a time commitment. You'll need to spend significantly more time supervising and training your new dogs, so time management can become an issue if you have other commitments in your life. Bringing home dogs that have already formed a close bond is great, but if you ever need to separate them, to go to the vet for example, the dogs may both react poorly. Dogs that have never been on their own may also be anxious and fearful and the one left at home could resort to destructive behavior. Housetraining is also much more difficult with multiple puppies. Bad habits are hard enough to break with one dog, but with two or more, it can be a serious challenge.

There are pros and cons to bringing home multiple puppies from the same litter, so consider this decision carefully before committing to it. Working full-time, plus family or hobby commitments, will leave you little time to work with more than one dog at a time. If you do decide that adopting littermates is the right decision, be sure to take each dog out alone on a regular basis to prevent separation anxiety and allow them to develop an individual sense of confidence. You must also train them together regularly so that when you need to take them somewhere as a group, you can keep them under control.

If you are hesitant about bringing home multiple puppies, but don't like the idea of your dog being alone, consider adopting a single Belgian Malinois first. Once he's been properly trained and socialized, you can consider bringing another into your home. With this method, your dog may only be alone for a few months, but you'll have enough time to establish the basics before shifting your focus to another dog.

Photo Courtesy of
Frank Davis
House of K9

Options if Your Pets Don't Get Along

It's entirely possible that you can spend an endless amount of time trying to convince your pets to get along, but they still won't like each other. Some animals may simply not be interested in making friends, especially if they're older or have been alone for a long time. Make sure that you aren't rushing your introductions and be sure to give animals plenty of time before reaching any conclusions. It can often take weeks or even months before some animals are willing to accept another pet into their lives. Patience is key, but so is a commitment to training. As a last resort, you might also consider seeking the advice of a professional.

If you've done everything you can and your pets still don't get along, you may need to make a serious decision. Giving up a beloved pet can be a heartbreaking decision, but managing pets that don't get along is a lifelong commitment that requires serious consideration. It will take a significant amount of time and effort to keep your pets separated while ensuring that each receives enough exercise, affection, and care. Each pet will require a safe and appropriately sized space to retreat to where the other cannot reach them. Managing separate pets is a lifestyle decision that can be stressful, exhausting, and time-consuming, so it's important that you consider whether you can provide this level of care for the duration of your pets' lives.

It's perfectly acceptable to admit that you are not willing or able to manage pets separately for their entire lives. No matter how much you love your pets, sometimes finding a more appropriate home for one of them is the best option. Some pets prefer single-pet environments, while others just need a different environment in order for them to be happy. This decision can be utterly heart-breaking, but it is your responsibility to make the best choices regarding your pets' wellbeing.

CHAPTER 12
Training Your Belgian Malinois

"As a new Malinois owner, your respect for your new partner should grow with time. The Malinois is smarter, faster, and more intense that most other dog breeds. If you can successfully use these attributes to your advantage during training you will see what the hype is about. A new owner should self educate as much as possible. If you do not, you will ruin your first dog and most likely end up blaming the dog for your failures as an owner. Self educate and seek professional help. All professional help is not equal, find someone with real working dog and Malinois experience. Do you want a Nissan mechanic changing the oil in your Ferrari? I don't."

MARK ROTH JR.
BlackJack Malinois

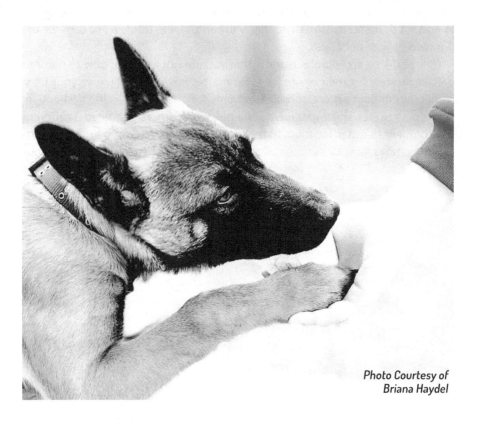

Photo Courtesy of
Briana Haydel

Benefits of Proper Training

Regular training sessions are a great way to prevent your Belgian Malinois from becoming bored and developing bad habits. Even sessions as short as five to ten minutes throughout the day can strengthen your bond with your dog and exercise both his mind and body. It's not uncommon for dogs to tire more quickly during training sessions than they would on a walk or during a play session. It's much more exhausting for your dog to use both his brain and his body than his body alone, so training sessions do not have to be lengthy to see the benefits. A Malinois who receives a satisfactory amount of physical and mental stimulation will be calmer and better behaved. A calm dog can also focus more easily, setting up your next session for success.

The commands you teach your Belgian Malinois will depend on what you plan on doing with him. If he will be an active family companion, the most basic obedience skills and a solid recall should be enough to keep him under control in most of the situ-

Photo Courtesy of Briana Haydel

ations you'll encounter with him. Of course, you can also teach him plenty of tricks to impress your friends and family. If you plan on competing with your Malinois in sports such as conformation, obedience, or any protection sport, your list of required commands will be longer. No matter what you choose to teach your dog, the benefits of proper training are nearly endless.

Operant Conditioning Basics

"You must be consistent and fair when training a Malinois. They learn behaviors quickly and they do not enjoy being drilled (doing the same behavior over and over during the same training session). A clever Malinois owner will make training sessions short and filled with fun."

SUSIE WILLIAMSON
Merson Belgian Malinois

Operant conditioning is one of the most common methods of learning used by professional trainers. It was originally promoted by American psychologist and behaviorist B.F. Skinner, who developed his theory based on the idea that humans and animals are too complex to learn only through classical conditioning. He suggested that if behaviors were followed with a positive experience, it was more likely that the learner would be willing to repeat the behavior in the future. If the behavior were followed with a negative experience, the learner would be discouraged from repeating the behavior again.

Skinner identified three environmental responses that he believed were responsible for shaping behavior: neutral operants, reinforcers, and punishments. Neutral operants were environmental responses that had no influence on whether the learner would be willing to repeat the behavior. An example of a neutral operant would be if you respond to your dog's behavior by describing the plot of your favorite movie. Your story is not likely to have any effect on whether your dog repeats the behavior in the future. Reinforcers can be positive or negative and increase the likelihood of the learner repeating the behavior. Examples of positive reinforcers include food, play, and affection. Negative reinforcers include the removal of an unpleasant sensation such as pressure on the leash. Punishments may range from simply unpleasant to painful. Minor punishments might include loud noises such as a clap or the word "No!" Painful punishments should be avoided at all costs as they can leave lasting damage on a dog's body and mind.

HELPFUL TIP
Training Tips

Belgian Malinois are very intelligent and eager to please, making them relatively easy to train. They do best with positive reinforcement—so reward your dog for doing what you want. Punishment or dominance-based training may make your Malinois aggressive.

Positive Reinforcement

In dog training, operant conditioning is found in the form of positive
reinforcement, which is the most popular training method among canine
professionals. Dogs are usually highly
motivated by both food and praise, so
they learn the quickest using positive
reinforcement. After the dog performs
a desired behavior, the trainer will
respond with treats, toys, or praise,
which will encourage the dog to repeat
the behavior in order to gain more
rewards. Positive reinforcement can
work against you, however, as many bad
habits are self-rewarding. For example,
if your Belgian Malinois shoves you out
of the way when you open your front
door and is rewarded with an exciting
romp around the neighborhood as you

Photo Courtesy of Lucinde Perdok

try to catch him, he's probably going to try it again. The same goes for getting into
the trash. If your Malinois knocks the trashcan over and gets to eat delicious left-
overs, he's more likely to repeat this behavior in the future. This is why managing
your dog's environment is so important. If you don't give your dog these opportunities in the first place, he'll never get to experience the rewards of being naughty.

Negative Reinforcement

Negative reinforcement is quite useful in dog training, but it is typically used
in combination with positive reinforcement to achieve better results. Though dogs
will learn through negative reinforcement alone, adding a reward will further
encourage them to perform the right behavior time and again. Many amateur
trainers frequently confuse negative reinforcement with punishments, giving the
method a bad rap. However, it can be quite useful when used correctly.

An example of correct negative reinforcement can be found in leash training.
Before leash training, most dogs will respond to pressure on the leash by pulling
in the opposite direction. To correct this, trainers will often put gentle pressure
on the leash and encourage the dog to move with the pressure instead of against
it by luring the dog with a tasty treat. The moment the dog steps in the right
direction the pressure on the leash is released and the dog is rewarded with the

treat. This removal of pressure at the right moment is negative reinforcement in action. If the dog steps backwards against the pressure on the leash, the trainer maintains the gentle pressure until the dog performs the right behavior. The leash pressure is not painful and is not a punishment, it's just a little unpleasant. With repetition, the dog will learn that if he gives in to the leash pressure instead of bracing against it, he can quickly make the pressure go away.

Punishments

Punishments differ from negative reinforcement in that they discourage the dog from repeating a behavior in the future. An example of a punishment might be seen when you catch your dog relieving himself on your living room rug. If this action is consistently met with a correction such as a loud clap, stomp, or "No!", it's unlikely that your dog will want to continue with this type of behavior.

When using punishments in your training, it's crucial that you never be harsher than you need to be. Kicking, hitting, or yelling at your dog will not teach him anything. Instead, he may react with fear or aggression if he feels he needs to protect himself from you. Punishments should not include anything that can cause lasting trauma. You want to use something that is unpleasant in the moment, but which your dog can walk away from without a problem. Claps, stomps, loud noises, or sprays of water are typically all it takes to correct inappropriate behavior.

Essential Commands

Belgian Malinois are incredibly intelligent dogs that are capable of learning an almost unlimited number of commands. There is no limit to what you can teach your new companion, but there are a few commands that are essential to any training program, no matter what you intend to do with your Malinois. Essential skills such as sit and down are useful for any dog and can be built upon to develop your dog's understanding of more advanced commands. It's also important for

FUN FACT
War Dogs

During World War I, Belgian Malinois served as messengers and assistants to the Red Cross and pulled ambulance carts and carts carrying firearms.

any dog to know how to walk politely on a leash, move off the furniture when asked, or give up a toy or other item upon request. If you intend to compete in dog sports with your Malinois, these commands will be the foundation for much of the training required in order to be successful in the show or competition ring.

Photo Courtesy of
Shayne Piront

Name Recognition

The first skill you should teach your Belgian Malinois in the first few days after bringing him home is name recognition. If your new companion had a name given to him in his previous home he may already respond to his name, but if he's particularly young or doesn't respond to the name he was given, you may need to teach him. This is an essential skill that is useful in all other aspects of training, so be sure to take the time to teach your dog how to recognize his own name.

Start by taking a handful of treats and gaining your Malinois' attention with them. Say your dog's name and immediately hand him a treat. Small training treats will work well, or you can use kibble, but you want to use something that will keep your dog's attention. Name recognition sessions don't need to be long, but the more frequently you can do it, the more quickly your dog will learn. Repeat the process of saying your dog's name and rewarding him and eventually he will understand that when you say his name, he should pay attention to you, especially since there might be something tasty if he does.

Sit

After name recognition, sit is typically the first command that is taught to most dogs, simply because it's easy for most dogs to learn. The sit command is useful in asking your dog to wait politely for his dinner, ride calmly in the car, or wait while you put his collar or harness on. It's also an essential skill in many dog sports.

Sit is taught best when your Malinois is wearing a collar and leash so that he cannot walk away from you should he get distracted or decide to wander off. You can teach this command using positive reinforcement alone or a combination of positive and negative reinforcement. It's up to you to decide which method will work best for you and your dog.

To use positive reinforcement only, wave a treat in front of your Malinois' nose to focus him. Once he realizes you have something delicious, raise the treat slightly above his head. The treat should be out of reach, but not so high that the dog is encouraged to jump after it. Most dogs will understand that sitting will put them in the right position to reach the treat. Be sure to reward your Malinois the moment his hind end touches the ground. As he begins to understand, you can introduce the verbal command while moving the treat into position.

If you would like to incorporate negative reinforcement into your training to encourage your dog further, you can perform the above method of teaching the sit with the addition of adding a bit of pressure on your dog's hind end with one hand. Some trainers also choose to use gentle upward pressure on the leash to encourage the dog to sit. Timing is crucial in negative reinforcement so be sure to release the pressure the moment your dog's rear end touches the ground.

Lie Down

Once your Belgian Malinois understands the sit command, you can move on to teaching him to lie down. This command is particularly useful in situations where you need your dog to rest calmly, such as while you have lunch at a local café or when you have guests visiting your home. It's also the foundation for tricks such as roll over or crawl and is required in many dog sports.

The lie down command is taught most easily by putting your Malinois into a sitting position. From there, you can lure him down to the ground with a treat. Most dogs will follow the treat down without lifting their rear end, but if your dog does stand up, you'll need to return him to the sitting position and try again. Be sure to reward him the very second his elbows touch the ground.

Negative reinforcement can be added by adding gentle downward pressure on the leash in addition to the luring motion with the treat. At first, you may need to release the pressure as soon as your dog begins to move downward, but you can progress to releasing the pressure when his elbows touch the ground. Treats should only be given once your dog is fully in the down position.

Stay

The stay command is an essential skill for any Malinois, whether he's an active family companion or a future show ring star. It can be useful in teaching your dog patience and is also a required skill in a variety of dog sports. However, it's important to note that many trainers differentiate between the stay command and the wait command. Stay is typically used when asking the dog to stay in position for a longer period of time and the dog is usually only released when the handler returns to the same position where he gave the command. Wait is often used for shorter periods, such as waiting for breakfast, and the dog can be released with the handler at a distance if necessary.

To teach these commands, ask your Malinois to sit, lie down, or stand, whichever you choose. Eventually, you can teach him to stay or wait in all positions but start with a single position until he understands. To begin with, simply hesitate a moment before rewarding him. As you ask him to stay in position for several seconds or longer, you can begin introducing the verbal command. If your dog moves out of position, do not punish him. Simply move him back into position and try again. Eventually, you can ask him to stay or wait and take a step back. As your dog gains experience, you can put more distance between yourself and him and ask him to stay or wait for longer periods of time. With enough practice, you may be able to place him into a stay while you leave the room. You can also add distractions such as rolling a ball across the floor or tossing treats around the room.

Recall

"A solid recall is the most important skill for any dog. That is the most important command for your Belgian Malinois. A good "leave it" command is almost as essential."

SUZANNE J BELGER
Desert Mountain Malinois

The recall, or come command, is one of the most important skills for any dog to learn and can even save your dog's life one day. A dog with a solid recall will drop everything to return to his owner, no matter what is happening around him. This command is useful anytime you plan on having your dog off-leash, whether in your home or in public.

The recall is best taught with two handlers, so if you have a dog-loving friend or family member, ask them to help. To start, practice in an area with few distractions such as a quiet room. If you're outside, make sure you're practicing in an enclosed area or are using a sufficiently long leash. Ask your helper to hold your dog a short distance away while you stand ready with treats. Say your dog's name to attract his attention if he's not already watching you. Once you have his attention, say "Come!" or "Come here!" and excitedly pat your legs or clap your hands to encourage your Malinois to run to you.

Photo Courtesy of Anne-Marie Stoltz

After you give the verbal command, your helper can release the dog and he can run to meet you. When he reaches you, praise him enthusiastically and give him plenty of treats. The more excited you can be, the more likely he is to run to you. Now you can repeat the actions of the helper while your helper calls your dog back. This game can be played back and forth, but be sure to keep sessions short so your dog doesn't lose focus. This is an important skill that he needs to stay focused on and excited about.

Off

Part of your training program should include teaching your Belgian Malinois how to behave in your home. An important part of this training should include teaching him to move off the furniture when asked. However, you must remember to differentiate this command from the one you use to ask your dog to lie down. If you use the word "down" for that command, use something like "off" when asking him to move off the sofa. It doesn't really matter what word you use as long as you are consistent.

There are a few different ways to approach this command. The first method is using positive reinforcement only and luring the dog off the furniture with a high value treat. As your dog moves his body toward the floor, give him the verbal command of your choice. Once all four paws are touching the floor, reward him with plenty of treats and praise.

If you would prefer to add a bit of negative reinforcement, you can also put a collar and leash on your dog and add gentle leash pressure in addition to luring him with the treat. Again, only reward him once all four paws are on the ground. If you've previously worked on your Malinois' leash skills, this may be easy for him to understand.

You can also apply pressure from behind your dog with your hand, but you must use caution if you don't know your new dog well yet. Some dogs may snap when such pressure is applied, so if your Malinois is still quite new to you or you think he may bite, it's best to opt for other methods. Using your hand to grab your dog's collar may have the same aggressive result, so use that method with extreme caution. As you teach your dog this command, it can be helpful for him to wear a drag line while in the house. A drag line is simply a light leash that can be dragged around for easy access when you need it. Do not leave your dog unattended with a drag line on, however, as he may chew or swallow it.

Drop It

Another command that is important in order to enforce the rules of your home is drop it. Whether your Malinois has picked up something inappropriate in your home or on a walk, you want him to give it up when asked. This command is also beneficial in preventing your dog from developing resource-guarding issues.

No matter what your Belgian Malinois has in his mouth, it's never advisable to remove the object with your hand. He may clamp his jaws down and refuse to let go or he may even snap at you. Instead, it's best to trade him for something of higher value than what he already had. You may need to use something different than your usual training treats for this, such as small bites of cheese or meat. Offer the treat to your dog, luring him some distance away from the object so that you can safely grab it. If it's an item he's allowed to have, such as a chew toy, you can return it and try again. As your Malinois learns to consistently drop the item, you can add a verbal command such as drop it or give.

Leave It

Whether you're walking your Belgian Malinois around the neighborhood or competing in dog sports, you don't want your dog to lose focus every time he smells something interesting. In order to prevent him from wandering off instead of listening to you, you'll want to teach him the leave it command. This command can be used to tell your dog to walk away from other dogs, someone else's dropped treats, or trash on the sidewalk and is an essential skill for any well-behaved canine.

Photo Courtesy of Sara Golac

Most trainers use a verbal command such as leave it or walk away for this skill, but you can use whatever word you choose. Be sure to carry plenty of high value treats with you to ensure your dog will want to focus on you instead of the distractions. You will also need to have your dog on a leash to ensure you can keep your dog away from anything that might be self-rewarding should he choose the distraction over you. When your dog gets distracted, simply wave a treat near him and give him the verbal command of your choice as he walks toward the treat. Just a step or two away from the distraction is enough to earn a reward at first, but you can reward him for larger distances as he progresses in his training.

Advanced Commands

Once your Belgian Malinois has mastered the basic commands, you can begin to increase the challenge in his daily training sessions. If you plan on showing him or competing in certain sports, you might consider teaching him sport-specific commands. Tricks can also be a fun way to bond with your dog and you can even compete in the AKC's new Trick Dog class if you choose. You can also increase the challenge of the commands he already knows, such as increasing the length of stays or the distance of recalls. You can ask your dog to sit on top of objects such as tree stumps or benches or try walking him through a busy area of town while maintaining a loose leash.

No matter what you choose to teach your Malinois, it's crucial that you keep your training sessions as short and sweet as possible. In the beginning, this may mean sessions as short as three to five minutes. If you go beyond what your dog's attention span can handle, you risk frustrating him, and he may begin to dread your training session. Rather than risk upsetting him, keep each session short and always end on a good note. If your Malinois seems to be struggling with a certain task, return to something he knows well for a few repetitions to boost his confidence and end the lesson there. You want to keep your dog happy and engaged, so it's important that he feels good about himself after every session.

CHAPTER 13
The Belgian Malinois in Work and Sport

"When it comes to training, the Belgian Malinois is like no other! They are considered the elite in many fields. They learn extremely quickly and easily, which is both good and bad. They pick up on everything you do including your mistakes so be careful when starting your training."

BETH ROOD
Roodhaus Belgian Malinois

Photo Courtesy of
Timothy Dobbins

The Working Belgian Malinois

A working dog is defined as a dog trained to perform specific, practical tasks. Working dogs differ from companion animals in that they have a particular job to perform, but there is no standard set of tasks that working dogs must be trained to do. The tasks taught to a working dog will depend on his job. For example, service and therapy dogs will need vastly different skills than police, military, or detection dogs. Herding dogs that work daily on their handler's farm are also considered working dogs.

Though Belgian Malinois are popular choices for military and police handlers, they are less commonly used as service or therapy dogs. Unfortunately, few Malinois are suited for this line of work. Though they are trainable and can easily learn the necessary commands, therapy and service dogs need to be calm with a stable temperament. The high energy and intense drive of the Malinois are not favored traits for dogs working with people in need of therapy or assistance. This is not to say it's impossible for a Malinois to excel in these sorts of jobs, but the breed is best suited for other types of work.

The Belgian Malinois may have originally been developed as a working farm dog, but few are used for that purpose today. Fewer people earn a living from farming in modern times, so the usefulness of the breed as herding dogs has all but disappeared. As with service and therapy dogs, there are breeds that are better suited to that line of work than the Malinois, so even on the farms remaining around the world, it's likely you'll see breeds like the Border Collie or Australian Cattle Dog. However, there are a few remaining breed fanatics who still use the breed for its original purpose so you may be able to see Malinois competing in herding competitions alongside the more popular herding breeds.

Some trainers consider their sport dogs to be working dogs, while others would categorize sport dogs differently than those trained to do more practical work. However, regardless of what job or sport a Belgian Malinois is trained to do, the dogs can still be considered canine athletes and should be treated as such.

FUN FACT

A Long History as Police Dogs

A notice in the January 1908 issue of the AKC Gazette mentioned that five Belgian Sheepdogs had been added to the New York City police force. Now, the Malinois is one of the most popular police dog breeds in the United States.

The Belgian Malinois and Dog Sports

Belgian Malinois have been described as perpetual motion machines. They are active and ready to work around the clock. Combined with the breed's incredible intelligence, the Malinois is an ideal dog for a variety of sports. The benefits of competing in sports with your Malinois go both ways. Not only will your new dog excel in any sport you choose, but the sport itself is a great way of providing the physical and mental exercise needed to prevent your Malinois from getting bored and developing bad habits.

Although Malinois were originally bred as all-around farm and herding dogs, they now excel in many different dog sports. If you attend any canine competition where speed, athleticism, and intelligence are favored, you're bound to see a Malinois there. Though they have gained fame from their success in protection sports such as IPO and French Ring, Malinois can also be found competing in everything from obedience and agility to dock diving and scent work.

Photo Courtesy of Hannah Meers

Protection Sports

"The Belgian Malinois is extremely smart. Over 30 years of training under my belt, I've found that this breed is second only to the Border Collie in their keen sense of catching onto a lesson the first or second time it's taught to them. The Malinois willingness to learn, and their sensitivity to their owner (handler), makes this breed a force in many areas - this would include obedience, protection work, herding, drug detection, as well as search and rescue. The Malinois is quite a package."

RAYMOND FARBER
Farbenholt Kennels

If you're unfamiliar with canine protection sports, these unique dog sports have been designed to test a dog's ability to protect not only himself, but his handler as well. It's a common misconception that training for protection sports will make a dog aggressive, but this simply isn't true. All protection sports test the temperament of a dog, not just his ability to protect. Aggressive dogs simply will not pass the test. Protection dogs must be safe around their handlers as well as the general public. These dogs possess incredible self-control and only react aggressively when the situation calls for it, such as when the handler is threatened.

Many protection sports simulate situations a dog may encounter as a working police or military dog. However, training a Malinois to compete in protection sports will not result in a dog that can go from competition directly into a position as a military or police canine. If the intent is for the dog to become a working Malinois, he will need additional job specific training. Knowing what type of sport your new dog's parents or siblings competed successfully in may be of help to a handler seeking a future working Belgian Malinois.

There are five different protection sports:

Belgian Ring

Belgian Ring is one of the oldest and most difficult protection sports and is entirely dominated by Belgian Malinois. While other breeds are technically permitted, they do not participate because they have little chance of besting a Malinois in competition. Most Belgian Ring competitions in Europe are held by the Nationaal Verbond der Belgische Kynologen (NVBK), which are judged by the approximately 50 NVBK-approved judges. The sport is divided into three levels, each increasing in difficulty compared to the last. Competition is stiff as only about 100 dogs receive Level III certification each year.

Photo Courtesy of
Derrick Lee

Malinois competing in Belgian Ring are judged on their obedience, jumping ability, and bite work. In the obedience phase of competition, dogs are tested on their ability to follow the handler both on and off leash. They must perform a variety of commands including sit, down, and stand. Stay commands are given and the dog is expected to stay in place while the handler walks out of the dog's sight. Dogs are also required to retrieve an object that is to be thrown by the handler, but only once the handler gives the command to fetch the object. Additionally, the handler is given a wooden stick, which he or she places among similar-looking sticks. The dog must then retrieve the correct stick based on the presence of the handler's scent on the stick.

The jumping phase requires Malinois to jump a wooden fence that is approximately 7.5 feet in height. This may seem like an incredible feat, and it is, but the Malinois competing in this difficult sport are more than capable of this type of athletic endeavor. They're also required to jump over a hedge measuring about four feet in height, after which they must wait politely until their handler calls them back over the hedge. A canal or similar obstacle measuring up to 14 feet in length must also be jumped on command.

The bite work phase is one of the most difficult as it requires the dog to possess incredible courage as well as trainability. This is where the dog's temperament is thoroughly tested. From a distance, a helper dressed in a bite suit attracts the dog's attention through aggressive body language. The handler releases the dog with the appropriate command so that he can then bite the helper. Depending on the judges' preference, the dog may also need to clear an obstacle on his way to the helper. Once the dog's jaws are firmly locked onto the bite suit, the helper then attempts to intimidate the dog by spraying him with water or hitting him with a stick. The stick is usually made of a material such as bamboo so it makes a clattering noise but will break easily if too much pressure is applied. The aim is to intimidate the dog, not injure him. The handler then approaches the dog and helper and calls the dog to him, at which point the dog must release immediately and return to the side of the handler. After the dog is called off, he must walk politely alongside the handler and helper, and wait while the two humans shake hands. The dog is not to react aggressively during this time. Only after the helper "attacks" the handler can the dog react protectively.

Malinois are also required to search for and find a helper after a blank gunshot is fired. While firing the gun, the helper hides behind one of many blinds and the dog is given the command to search. After the dog locates the helper, he is not to attack him, but he must bark and guard him until the handler arrives to call the dog off. Once the dog is called to the handler's side, he must then walk politely alongside the handler and helper until the helper attempts to "escape," at which point the dog will bite and hold until the handler arrives once again to call him off.

Photo Courtesy of
Samuel Castañón

Additionally, Malinois competing in Belgian Ring are required to guard an object from a helper in a bite suit, who will attempt to take whatever it is the dog is guarding. The helper may also try to intimate or distract the dog by waving sticks at him or using water or toy balls to draw his attention away from the object he's supposed to protect. This is performed with the dog wearing a muzzle as well as without.

Finally, throughout the field where the dog will be working, distractions are put in place in an attempt to lure the dog away from his work. Generally, meat is used for this purpose and dogs are required to ignore it during all phases of the competition.

French Ring

French Ring is similar to Belgian Ring in that the required tasks are about the same, though jumps are typically not quite as high or as long as in Belgian Ring. French Ring is also split into three different levels of difficulty and dogs must pass an initial test for sociability, temperament, and aptitude before they're allowed to proceed in the higher levels of competition. Nearly all work is performed off leash and with no collar. Like Belgian Ring, once the dog and handler enter the field, they perform all phases of the competition before leaving the field. This can take anywhere from 40 minutes to 1 hour. The various phases of the competition are performed in a specific order: jumping, obedience, then bite work. However, judges are to determine the specific layout of the field and order of the exercises within each phase.

KNPV (Koninklijke Nederlands Politiehond Vereniging)

KNPV is similar to both French and Belgian Ring in the tasks required but is more geared toward the development of working police dogs. KNPV competitions are also only found in the Netherlands. Dogs can earn the titles of PH 1 (Politiehond 1 or Police Dog 1), PH 2, Obj. Bew. (Object Bewakingshond or Object Protection Dog), Basis Zoekhonden (Basic Search Dog), and Zoekhonden (Zoekhond, Sorteerhond, and Reddingshond or Search Dog, Detection Dog, and Rescue Dog). KNPV dogs must also attempt to stop a helper who tries to escape by bicycle, as well as one that fires a blank from a gun and throws various objects at the dog in order to deter him. These are all essential skills of a police dog, so dogs are judged accordingly.

Mondio Ring

Although the exercises required in Mondio Ring are similar, this sport is less structured than the other Ring sports. It was created to combine the best aspects of all the other protection sports and is rising in popularity around the world. Unlike

Photo Courtesy of Dionne Cancino

French and Belgian Ring, helpers are not allowed to hit the dog with the stick, just wave it around him to intimidate. Competition is again divided into three levels of difficulty, as well as an initial temperament test prior to competing in Mondioring Level I. Trials are set up according to a theme and props, scenarios, and distractions are placed throughout the competition field. The exercises remain the same from trial to trial, but the theme is left to the judges' discretion. This prevents two trials from ever being the same, eliminating the possibility of a dog being prepared by rote.

Schutzhund, or IPO

Schutzhund, or IPO, is a German dog sport originally created to test the working abilities of German Shepherds. Though the sport is still dominated by German Shepherds, many Malinois compete successfully. Schutzhund differs from other protection sports as it replaces the jumping or agility phase with tracking. The track is a minimum of 600 to 900 feet in length with two articles or pieces of cloth placed within the track. There must be at least two legs and three corners within the track as well. The articles must be at least 20 minutes old and are laid in place by the handler prior to starting. Competing dogs have 15 minutes to solve the track and find the articles. Schutzhund also differs from other protection sports in that the three phases are performed separately, rather than at one time. The obedience and protection phases of Schutzhund take only eight to ten minutes each.

Dogs competing in IPO must pass a temperament test prior to competing in the three levels of Schutzhund. In IPO, more emphasis is placed on the quality of bite work than in other protection sports. The dog's grip is taken into account, whereas in the other sports, as long as the dog does not let go he will receive full points. Precision is also valued, so IPO judges tend to favor the heavy but precise nature of the German Shepherd over the flashy lightweight nature of the Malinois. During the search for the helper, Schutzhund dogs are expected to search in a specific pattern, unlike other sports where the dog may search as he pleases. Dogs are also required to heel on the left side of the handler. In Schutzhund, it's not about just getting the job done, but about how the job gets done.

Herding

Although few Malinois are used as full-time herding dogs these days, many still possess the natural instinct needed to excel in modern herding competitions. The American Kennel Club requires all dogs that intend to compete in herding pass an instinct test prior to entering into competition. No training is involved in the instinct test, but dogs are judged on their reaction to the presence of livestock while remaining on a 6-15 foot leash or long line. The dogs are evaluated on how interested they are in the stock, whether they are responsive to guidance, how forcefully they handle the stock, and whether they adjust their position to the herd. Whether or not they bark and the manner in which they approach the stock are also key elements of the instinct test. Once approved by two separate judges, the dog will receive a certificate allowing him to pursue the Herding Tested (HT) title.

To gain the HT title, the dog must once again be approved by two separate judges. In this test, two pylons or markers are place on the centerline of a fenced arena, one at each end. Stock are typically held at one end of the arena near a pylon before the dog begins working. All herding dogs must enter the arena on leash and once the judge deems the dog safe to be around the livestock, the lead can be removed. Both timing and testing begin the moment the lead is removed. Often, the dog is asked to remain in place while the handler moves to a more appropriate position in relation to the livestock. The dog is then tasked with moving the stock to the other end of the arena, around the other pylon, and then back toward their original position.

The five elements of the test that are evaluated by the judge consist of a controlled pause at the beginning as well as two changes in direction while exhibiting controlled movement of the livestock. The dog must then stop on command and once the stock has been returned to their original position, the dog must leave the stock and come to the handler when called. All of this must be completed in under ten minutes.

There is also a Pre-Trial Test, in which any dogs can compete regardless of whether they have a Herding Tested title. However, many participants recommend pursuing the HT title first to gain knowledge in the sport before attempting a Pre-Trial Test. Like the HT trial, dogs are allowed ten minutes to get the job done. The dog must move stock from one area of an arena to the opposite side, where a pen for the stock is located. This time, the five elements that the dog will be judged on include a stay or controlled pause as well as controlled passage of the stock that includes a single change of direction and clearance of four gates. There must also be one stop on the course as well an additional stop while the handler opens the pen gate. The penning of the stock is the final element.

Once a dog successfully passes the Pre-Trial Test, he can enter into herding trials, which are separated into categories of difficulty: Started, Intermediate, and Advanced. Herding trials are similar to previous tests but vary in the obstacles that the dog must negotiate with the herd. The final title that can be earned in these competitions is Herding Advanced (HX). Once a dog has earned this title as well as 15 championship points in Advanced classes, he can be awarded the title of Herding Champion.

Obedience

"Even if you do not have a specific need for formal training getting your Malinois involved in training or a dog sport that it excels at can be a great way to build a bond while physically and mentally exercising the dog. Often times, I have seen a handler bring a new pup to a sport club with no intensions of getting fully involved. The next thing you know the same handler has made new friends, is meeting with the club a few times a week, and has title his or her dog. Getting involved in a sport your dog excels in will keep you interested and can be very rewarding."

MARK ROTH JR.
BlackJack Malinois

Obedience trials are among the AKC's most popular dog sport classes. They demonstrate a dog's ability to follow specified routings and emphasize the dog's usefulness as a companion animal. The objective of this competition is to exhibit the dog's ability to behave himself and obey commands not only at home, but in public and around strange people and other dogs. Accuracy and precision are highly valued in this sport. Knowing this about the sport makes it easier to understand why Belgian Malinois are so successful. They are intelligent, intuitive, and dedicated to their work, making them ideal dogs for obedience competition.

The commands required in obedience will vary according the level of competition. Lower levels are performed on leash, while more advanced classes require all work to be done off leash. Dogs are asked to sit, lie down, stay, heel, retrieve dumbbells, jump over obstacles, and come when called. Although these seem like basic commands, they are combined in competition to present a level-appropriate challenge to competitors.

In Novice classes, dogs must receive three qualifying scores under two separate judges before earning the title of Companion Dog (CD). They can then compete in the Open class, where the challenge is increased through the use of off leash work, retrieving, and jumping challenges. Again, dogs must earn three qualifying scores under two different judges before being awarded the title of Companion Dog Excellent (CDX).

The most challenging obedience class is the Utility class, which also includes scent discrimination, jumping, silent signal exercises, and directed retrieves. The same qualifications must be met as in previous classes in order to earn the Utility Dog (UD) title. Beyond that, dogs must qualify in both the Open and Utility

*Photo Courtesy of
Chandra Martinez*

classes on the same day in order to earn the coveted Utility Dog Excellent (UDX) title. The highest obedience title a dog can earn is the Obedience Trial Champion (OTCH). To earn this title, dogs must receive 100 points, a first place in both Open B and Utility B, plus one more first place in either class, but other qualifying points do not need to come through 1st place wins. One dog each year is given the title of AKC National Obedience Champion (NOC). To be invited to compete for this title, dogs must be one of the top three obedience Malinois for the year.

Agility

Belgian Malinois are known for being fast and agile, so it's no surprise to see them in the winner's circle at any agility event. Agility requires dogs and their handlers to navigate a course of obstacles as quickly as possible. There is a time limit, known as the "standard course time," and any dog that goes over this time will incur time faults. Further penalties can be incurred if dogs knock down any bars from the jumps, go off course, or refuse an obstacle. The fastest dog with the fewest penalties wins. As dogs must perform off leash, it's up to handlers to guide their dog through the course using only their voice and hand signals. Touching the dog or the obstacles is forbidden and will result in penalties.

The obstacles encountered in the agility ring vary according the organization holding the competition. One of the most common obstacles encountered is the A-frame, which is a triangular obstacle made of two ramps hinged together and raised to a height of between five and six feet. The bottoms of each ramp are painted a different color to indicate a "contact zone," where the dog must place at least one paw while climbing on and off the obstacle.

A similar obstacle is known as the dog walk, which is a raised 12-foot plank with ramps on either end. The center plank is raised to a height of about four feet, but the exact height depends on the regulations of the organization holding the competition. The dog walk also features contact zones on the ramps on either side of the center plank. The seesaw is a 10- to 12-foot plank that pivots on a slightly off-center fulcrum, similar to a seesaw found on a child's playground. The reason for the pivot point being off-center is to allow the same side to return to the ground, setting the obstacle up for the next competitor. In some organizations, this is also accomplished by weighing one side down slightly. However, the plank must be balanced in a way that allows even the smallest dogs to descend to the ground on the high end of the seesaw.

There are also a variety of jumps consisting of horizontal bars, panels, or hoops. Jumps are adjusted to accommodate the different size classes, so jumps will be higher for a Belgian Malinois than they would be for a Chihuahua. Weave poles are one of the more exciting obstacles, as dogs must weave their way through a series of six to twelve upright poles. Dogs must always enter weave poles with the first pole to the left, otherwise they will receive a penalty. A pause table or box is a raised table or taped-off square where a dog must sit or down for a designated period of time, usually about five seconds. Though some organizations may feature other obstacles, these are the basics found in most agility competitions.

Other Sports

The Belgian Malinois is a highly competitive breed that excels in nearly any dog sport. In addition to the sports listed previously in this chapter, it's not uncommon to see Malinois competing in sports such as dock diving, flyball, canicross, nose work, and even weight pulling. With a breed as athletic and intelligent as the Malinois, you should be able to train your Malinois to compete in nearly any dog sport, so don't be afraid to try something new. Here are just a few sports to consider:

Dock Diving

In this unique water sport, dogs compete by doing just what the name implies. Each dog in competition gets the chance to jump off a dock or platform into a pool of water to see which dog can jump the farthest. Handlers encourage the dogs to jump as far as possible by giving the dogs a running start and tossing a floating toy out over the water. The dog that covers the most distance before hitting the water wins.

Flyball

In this team sport, dogs run one at a time over a series of hurdles to reach a box containing a tennis ball. As they reach the box, dogs must press the spring-loaded pad on the front of the box to release the ball. They must then run back over the hurdles to the start line, where their teammates are awaiting their turn. Teams consist of four dogs and the first team to have all four dogs cross the finish line with no fallen hurdles or dropped balls win.

Canicross

This sport is ideal for owners who want to stay as fit as their dogs. Canicross originally began in Europe as a way of keeping sled dogs fit through the off season. Runners can compete with one or two dogs. The dogs wear harnesses specially designed for pulling or mushing and are attached by bungee leashes to a belt worn around the runner's waist. The bungee cord reduces the impact from pulling on both the dog and runner. The runners than compete against each other in the same manner as any other dog-free foot race. Distances vary according to the individual competition and the fastest team of runner and dog wins.

Nose Work

This relatively new sport is designed to mimic work done by professional detection dogs. Dogs must search indoor or outdoor spaces, or vehicles, for specific scents such as birch, anise, or clove oil. As with detection dogs, competing canines must signal to their handler once they've detected one of the specific scents. This sport is rising in popularity due to its accessibility for dogs and handlers. Senior and disabled dogs are able to compete alongside young and fit dogs, just as long as they are able to signal the presence of the scents.

Weight Pulling

Though most popular among bully breeds and Nordic sled dog breeds, weight pulling is becoming increasingly popular with all breeds regardless of their original purpose. Dogs compete to pull carts or sleds across short distances of snow, gravel, grass, or carpet. They are fitted with harnesses designed to distribute weight evenly across their chests to reduce injury. Dogs are categorized into classes by weight and the dog that pulls the most weight in each class wins.

Treibball

This exciting sport was developed as a way of allowing herding breeds to express their natural herding instinct in a more urban livestock-free environment. Dogs are trained to move large exercise balls into a soccer-type goal. The object of the sport is to move eight balls into the goal in a set time period, typically 15 minutes. The dog and handler team that can herd the balls into the goal in the fastest period of time wins.

CHAPTER 14
Nutrition

*"Find a quality food for your Malinois. Think of your dog as an athlete...
an athlete wouldn't eat at McDonald's every day, so make sure you feed your
BM a dog food that has all he/she needs."*

RAYMOND FARBER
Farbenholt Kennels

The Importance of a Balanced Diet

In order for your Belgian Malinois to grow and develop properly, a balanced and nutritious diet is crucial. Without the right nutrients in your dog's diet, he is at risk of developing serious and even life-threatening health problems. Although a balanced diet is important for adult dogs, it's particularly essential that growing puppies receive the right balance of fats, carbo-

HELPFUL TIP
Diet Is Key

Always discuss your dog's diet with your vet, but typically, athletic dogs like the Belgian Malinois do well on a high-protein diet. Your dog needs protein to build muscle, and an active Mal should have more muscle than the average dog.

hydrates, proteins, and amino acids so that they may grow into healthy adults. Unfortunately, the signs of an unbalanced diet will not be immediately obvious. You won't see the effects of incorrect nutrition for several weeks or even months, and these effects are often permanent, especially in puppies.

A balanced diet is both a precise combination of nutrients and an ideal number of calories for your Belgian Malinois. Obesity is a serious and common health problem in domestic dogs, so make sure that portion control is as much a part of your dog's diet as what he's actually eating. Remember, puppies and active adults will need to consume more food and more calories than senior or sedentary dogs. Though many brands of dog food will have a suggested feeding amount listed on the bag or container, this is a general suggestion and should not be followed to the letter. As a dog ages, he will need his diet changed frequently to reflect the changes to his lifestyle, so remember to periodically evaluate your Malinois' diet and make any necessary alterations. If you're still unsure of how much your new companion should be eating, or you're unsure of what an ideal body condition looks like for your dog, consult your veterinarian or canine nutritionist for advice.

While shopping for dog food, you'll likely notice that a large number of pet food companies advertise their products as appropriate for all life stages. While this may be true for some dogs, others may need a more specialized diet, especially active working breeds such as the Belgian Malinois. You may find yourself switching your dog to different recipes or brands to adapt to the changes he'll undergo throughout his life. It's unlikely that your dog will be able to eat the same type of food for his entire life, so be prepared to adapt as needed.

Basic Nutrition

Most pet owners, and even veterinary professionals, choose to learn only the basics of canine nutrition. Nutrition is such a complex topic that even dedicated canine nutritionists spend their lives studying the way we feed our dogs and how we can improve it in order to better the lives of the animals we care for. This section will cover only the basic concepts of nutrition, so if you have any further questions or would like to seek the advice of a professional, the American College of Veterinary Nutrition (ACVN) has published a list of board-certified veterinary nutritionists on their website. Though your veterinarian may also be able to answer basic nutrition questions, it's unlikely they'll have the expertise to address more complex nutritional queries, so it's best to contact a specialist.

Proteins and Amino Acids

Amino acids are the organic compounds that combine to form proteins. When protein molecules are broken down during digestion, the amino acids are what remain. Those amino acids are then used by your dog's body to synthesize different protein molecules to aid in the growth, maintenance, and repair of cells. As an example of how much protein is needed, it's estimated that approximately 30 percent of your Belgian Malinois' daily protein intake goes toward maintaining the cells in his coat.

There are about 20 different amino acids that make up the various proteins in your dog's body. About half are produced internally, while the other half are provided by a balanced diet. The amino acids contained in your dog's diet are often referred to as "essential amino acids" because if the diet is lacking in even one, your dog's system will not be able to effectively form certain proteins.

The ten essential amino acids necessary in a dog's diet are:

- Arginine
- Histidine
- Isoleucine
- Leucine
- Lysine
- Methionine
- Phenylalanine
- Threonine
- Tryptophan
- Valine

Common foods such as meat, eggs, and dairy products are typically high in protein, providing your dog's body with the right balance of essential amino acids needed for protein synthesis. While plants are appropriate for a human diet, they tend to be quite low in protein and do not provide the amino acids necessary for

protein synthesis in a dog's body. For this reason, vegetarian and vegan diets are not biologically appropriate for dogs and should not be fed.

Fat and Fatty Acids

Fats are by far the most concentrated source of energy in your Belgian Malinois' diet. Fats also provide your dog's body with fatty acids, which are the building blocks for substances in the body responsible for cell growth and maintenance. Though similar to amino acids, fewer essential fatty acids must be provided by your dog's diet. Fats are also responsible for the absorption of the fat-soluble vitamins A, E, D, and K. Additionally, fats are thought to be more palatable than proteins, so high fat diets may be suitable for picky eaters.

The essential fatty acids necessary in a balanced diet are:

- Arachidonic acid
- Linoleic acid
- Linolenic acid

It's likely that you've heard of omega-3 and omega-6 fatty acids. In terms of your Malinois' diet, linoleic acid provides him with omega-6 fatty acids and linolenic acid provides omega-3 fatty acids. It's important for your dog's diet to contain the correct balance of fatty acids, so a proper diet will contain more omega-6 than omega-3 fatty acids. Usually, the ratio is about 4 to 1.

Carbohydrates

As more responsible pet owners turn to more species-appropriate diets, carbohydrates have become an area of dispute. While carbohydrates do provide dogs with some energy, there are more efficient sources of energy available and dogs do not necessarily require carbs in their diet. For this reason, many raw feeders opt to feed their dogs little to no grains or carb heavy vegetables. However, most kibbles and plenty of homemade diets are quite high in carbohydrates and many dogs tolerate this type of diet fine.

Carbohydrates are broken down by your dog's digestive system into glucose, providing his body with energy. Many sources of carbohydrates also provide your dog with additional nutrients like phytochemicals, antioxidants, and other minerals. Carbs are also a great source of dietary fiber. However, it should be noted that if you intend to feed your Malinois starchy carbohydrates, they will need to be well cooked in order to be digestible, or else they'll likely ferment in the large intestine.

Feeding Dogs at Different Life Stages

"Every Belgian Malinois is different when it comes to nutrition. Find what works good for your dog and stick with it. My 12 year old female has been on raw food and supplements for the past 6 years since having bladder stones and you could never tell she is 12 years old."

BETH ROOD
Roodhaus Belgian Malinois

As you might imagine, your Belgian Malinois' nutritional needs are likely to change throughout his life as he ages. As his body and lifestyle changes, you'll need to adjust his diet accordingly. You may have noticed that many of the foods on the shelves of your local pet store are labeled for dogs of all life stages. These foods have been balanced according to the Association of American Feed Control Officials' (AAFCO) standards, but many owners choose to tailor their dog's diets to their life stages instead.

As an example, when you first bring your Malinois puppy home, he will require a higher number of calories and a slightly different ratio of vitamins and minerals in order to nourish his developing body. Many owners choose to feed a food specifically formulated for puppies until their dogs are about a year old. As an adult, your dog may require changes in his diet according to his activity level. Feeding working dogs is different than feeding the average pet. This topic will be discussed later in this chapter. As your Malinois reaches his senior years, his caloric needs will drastically reduce, at which time you may consider switching him to a senior dog food. Additionally, dogs that have been spayed or neutered will usually require fewer calories than those that haven't been altered due to their slowed metabolism. Pregnant

Photo Courtesy of Sam Sciolino

and lactating females will also need different nutrients than the average adult dog in order to provide their puppies with the right nutrients for proper growth and development.

As you can see, no two dogs will have the same nutritional requirements, so it's important to feed your dog as an individual. If you have multiple dogs in your home, this may even mean feeding them different foods to accommodate their individual needs throughout their various stages of life.

Different Types of Commercial Food

Kibble is what usually comes to mind when the topic of commercial dog food is brought up. By far, kibble is the most popular and widely available type of commercial dog food because of its availability and the convenience of feeding it. It also comes in a nearly endless variety of formulas to suit dogs of every life stage, no matter their health needs. Whether your dog has food sensitivities, heart disease, or is a perfectly healthy puppy, there's a kibble formulated for dogs just like him. In addition to the popular protein options of beef, chicken, and lamb, you'll also be able to find novel proteins such as salmon and kangaroo. Many brands also make kibble designed for specific breeds or sizes of dogs. Kibbles designed to help dogs with health issues such as arthritis or kidney disease are also available, though usually only through a veterinarian.

There are an increasing number of dogs developing sensitivities or allergies to common carbohydrates in kibble such as corn, wheat, and soy, so many owners are also choosing to feed their dogs grain-free diets. In these diets, traditional grains are replaced by starchy carbs like potatoes and peas. It should be noted that some veterinarians advise against a grain-free diet due to the apparent correlation between this type of diet and dilated cardiomyopathy (DCM). Though the connection has not yet been proven, research is ongoing, and some veterinarians may prefer to err on the side of caution. If you have any concerns about the ingredients in your dog's food or would like to know more about DCM, be sure to ask your vet at your Malinois' next appointment or consult a professional canine nutritionist.

Kibble has risen in popularity because it's ideal for busy owners who may lack the time, knowledge, or disposable income to make their dogs' food at home. In the United States, commercial dog food is formulated to AAFCO standards, so there's no need to be concerned whether you're feeding your dog a balanced diet. It's also frequently the most budget friendly option, though prescription kibble diets designed to treat certain health problems may be more expensive, as are many types of limited-ingredient diets formulated for dogs with food sensitivities.

Canned dog food is another popular option for owners, especially those with older dogs or picky eaters. Canned food is softer and has a stronger smell than kibble, so it's ideal for senior dogs or those who may turn their nose up at kibble. It also contains more moisture, so it can be beneficial for dogs who don't drink enough water on their own. As with kibble, canned food is available in a huge variety of formulas to suit your dog's individual needs as well as your budget. Canned food is usually more calorie dense than kibble, however, so it's important to monitor your dog's weight closely and adjust his portions as needed. Unlike kibble, canned food doesn't scrape plaque and tartar off your dog's teeth as he eats it, so you may need to provide your dog with dental chews or more frequent professional dental cleanings if canned food is his only source of nutrition.

As more dog owners begin to consider their dogs as family members, rather than just pets, fresh-cooked dog food has risen in popularity. Again, commercial fresh food diets offer the convenience of a prepared and balanced diet with the ingredients of a homecooked meal. Fresh-cooked food is also soft, like canned food, so it may be a better option for picky eaters or dogs with dental issues. This type of diet is typically found in the refrigerated section of your local pet store and is packaged into rolls. The rolls can be sliced into meal-sized portions and stored in your fridge until the next meal. Though fresh-cooked dog food is not the most expensive commercial option available, it does usually cost more than many brands of kibble or canned food.

In recent years, an increasing number of pet owners are seeking the benefits of feeding their dogs species-appropriate diets, but they may lack the time or knowledge required to make these types of diet at home. Commercial raw diets are typically found in the freezer section of your local pet store and are available in a variety of proteins and portion sizes. The nuggets or patties are made from a nutritionally balanced blend of meat, organs, bones, and fruits or vegetables. Like canned food, commercial raw diets can have a detrimental effect on your dog's dental health over time, so many raw feeders supply their dogs with the occasional recreational chew such as a knuckle or marrow bone to help clean their teeth. Some owners also supplement their dog's raw diet with goat milk or bone broth in order to provide a wider variety of nutrients. Commercial raw diets can be quite expensive, especially with a breed as large and active as the Belgian Malinois, so be sure that you budget accordingly.

Homemade Diets

"Raw diets are popular in the working dog world. They are great if you have the time and resources. I personally feed a raw diet supplemented by a quality kibble. Supplementing with kibble can save time and prep time while still allowing you to get some of the benefits of a raw diet. One of the main things I find important in a Malinois diet is consistency. Find something that works for you and stick with it."

MARK ROTH JR.

BlackJack Malinois

If you're interested in having full control over your Belgian Malinois' diet, you may be interested in feeding him a homemade diet. Before you commit to this decision, it's important to be aware that depending on where you live and the ingredients you use, a homemade diet may be more expensive than a commercial diet. Making your own dog food also requires a significant time commitment, so be sure that you're willing to dedicate the appropriate amount of time to meal preparation. While commercial diets are required to meet nutritional standards, usually according to AAFCO, it's solely your responsibility to make sure your dog's homemade diet is nutritionally balanced. As discussed previously, any imbalances in your Malinois' diet may not be apparent for some time and permanent damage is always possible.

If you're unsure whether you will be able to balance your dog's food, it's best to seek the advice of a certified canine nutritionist. The American College of Veterinary Nutrition (ACVN) has a list of board-certified veterinary nutritionists available on their website. Nutritionists typically formulate their recommended diets according to AAFCO or the National Research Council (NRC). Most are more than happy to work around any health problems, food sensitivities, ingredient availability, or budgetary concerns.

Raw diets are the most popular type of homemade diet and can usually be categorized as either Prey Model Raw (PMR) or Biologically Appropriate Raw Food (BARF). PMR diets are designed to simulate the diet of a wild dog and use estimated percentages of the meat, bone, and organ contained in a prey animal. Usually, this consists of about 80% muscle meat, 10% bone, and 10% organ, though these percentages may be adjusted to each dog's individual nutritional needs. Some PMR diets include a small amount of fruits and vegetables, but most do not.

The second category of raw diet, BARF, is similar to PMR diets, but BARF diets often allow for a higher percentage of vegetables and may also include starchy carbohydrates. Many raw feeders, both PMR and BARF, also supplement their dogs' diets with goat milk, fermented fish stock, or bone broth to provide additional nutrients. Bones in both diets may also be ground or processed, or the dog may chew them up on his own. It's important to note that many raw diets based strictly on percentages may be lacking in nutrients such as vitamin E, zinc, or manganese, so it's best to consult a canine nutritionist to help formulate a recipe for a balanced diet appropriate for your individual dog.

Cooked diets are also popular among owners who choose to make their dogs' food at home. They are ideal for dogs or owners who are unable or unwilling to tolerate a raw diet. They are also ideal for families with immunocompromised family members who should not be exposed to any potential pathogens contained in raw meat. The ingredients used in cooked diets resemble those in raw diets, but they are usually baked or boiled before feeding. Cooked diets also often contain starchy carbohydrates such as barley or rice. While some nutritional value may be lost during the cooking process, it's possible to make up for that loss with nutritional supplements such as kelp, dairy products, and vitamin mixtures. It's important to remember that cooked bones should never be fed, as they can splinter and harm your dog. In place of the bones present in most raw diets, you may provide your dog with essential calcium through the addition of ground eggshells, seaweed calcium, or a calcium supplement.

When making your dog's food at home, it's crucial that all safety precautions are taken in order to keep your dog and your family safe. As previously mentioned, raw bones do not shatter the way that cooked bones do, but hard weight-bearing bones, such as leg bones, may put your dog at risk of chipping or breaking a tooth. Although many owners use these types of bones as recreational chews without incident, it may spell trouble for heavy chewers. You should always monitor your dog when giving him any bones so that you can intervene should anything happen. Some dogs are also notorious "gulpers" who would rather swallow their food whole rather than chew it. With these types of dogs, it's recommended to only provide them with ground bones or bones that are large enough they can't even attempt to swallow them.

When feeding a homemade diet, it's your responsibility to make sure your dog's diet is not only nutritionally balanced but safe. Similarly, it's important to keep your family safe from any potential dangers involved with feeding a homemade diet. Though the incidents of sickness in the homes of raw feeders is nearly zero, it's important to follow proper hygiene protocols when feeding your dog raw meat. Clean your prep area as you normally would when working with raw meat and restrict your dog's access to your house during mealtimes. Many owners choose to feed their dogs in their kennels to limit the dogs' ability to carry raw meat or bones throughout the house, potentially spreading bacteria onto hard to clean surfaces like carpet or furniture. Some owners may choose to wipe their dog's face or paws after eating to help limit the spread of germs, while others choose not to accept kisses for a while after meals.

Weight Management

According to the Association of Pet Obesity Prevention, about 52 percent of adult dogs in the United States are considered overweight or obese. More than 90 percent of these owners do not recognize that their dogs are overweight. Though one of the most common health problems among all breeds of dogs, obesity can severely impact your dog's ability to enjoy life. It can lead to a multitude of other health problems, including joint problems like arthritis. While it may be tempting to give your dog a tasty treat every time he gives you those puppy eyes, for the sake of his health you need to resist. While you should keep a close eye on your dog's weight at home, you should also consider asking your veterinary about your Belgian Malinois' weight whenever he's due for a checkup. Though there is a recommended weight range for the breed, not all individuals will be at a healthy weight in this range. A healthy weight will depend on the dog's physical size, so although two Malinois may weigh the same, it's possible for one to be thin while the other is overweight if they differ significantly in height.

Portion size is one of the most important factors in keeping your Malinois at a healthy weight. In addition to feeding him the right amount of food at each meal, don't forget to calculate the calories involved in his daily amount of training treats and edible chews. You might forget about that handful of treats given during a training session, but your dog's waistline won't. If you're concerned about your dog's weight, you might also consider trading his high calorie treats for healthy options such as vegetables. Fruit is also a good option but should be fed in moderation due to the high sugar content.

As an active, high-energy breed, most Belgian Malinois are more than happy to burn off those extra calories with an extra-long walk or game of fetch. The more calories your dog burns, the more he'll be able to consume, so if you're unwilling to restrict his food, be sure to exercise him more. In addition to keeping your Malinois at a healthy weight, more physical activity will help keep him physically and mentally fit. A tired Malinois is less likely to engage in boredom-induced bad behaviors, so don't be afraid to keep your dog as busy and active as possible.

Food Allergies and Intolerances

As you decide on what to feed your new Belgian Malinois, it's important to keep an eye on how your dog tolerates any new foods you introduce into his diet. It's estimated that about ten percent of all allergies diagnosed in dogs are food allergies, so although the rate is quite low, it's important to understand what to look out for. Allergic reactions are due to a reaction by your dog's immune system in response to certain proteins in his diet. Intolerances, on the other hand, typically appear as digestive upset or an inability to digest certain ingredients. One of the most common symptoms of allergies is severe itching, usually all over the body rather than in one particular area. Depending on the severity of an allergic reaction, your dog may also experience hot spots, ear or skin infections, vomiting, and diarrhea. Common causes of allergic reactions or digestive upset include beef, lamb, chicken, corn, wheat, and soy.

Diagnosing a food allergy or intolerance is not a simple task. Though tests are available through your local veterinarian, the results are not completely reliable. Most veterinarians recommend an elimination diet instead to help determine the specific protein or proteins that are causing the problem. Elimination diets consist of feeding your dog a limited ingredient diet, usually with a novel protein such as salmon or kangaroo. Novel proteins are assumed to be a safe place to start as few dogs have developed a reaction to them. After enough time has passed for the symptoms to ease, new proteins are added one at a time while the dog is monitored for reactions. Each protein should be fed for several weeks before it's determined to be safe.

If you introduce a certain ingredient into your dog's diet and he begins itching or displaying signs of digestive problems, you'll know that protein is one you'll need to eliminate from your dog's diet. It's important to note that when performing an elimination diet, your dog cannot have any treats or snacks outside of his restricted diet. If you want to feed him treats, try using his food or search for treats with ingredients that complement his limited ingredient diet.

If the specific cause of the reaction cannot be determined, your veterinarian may recommend a hypoallergenic diet, which is usually only available by prescription. Commercial hypoallergenic diets are formulated with hydrolyzed proteins, which are proteins that have been broken down into sizes that are less likely to upset the immune system. Prescription diets are often quite expensive, so you may want to consider using an elimination diet first before resorting to a hypoallergenic diet.

Working Dog Nutrition

If your Belgian Malinois is heavily involved in dog sports or is far more active than the average pet, his nutritional needs are going to be different from those of a dog who only takes casual walks around the neighborhood. Canine athletes require a different nutrient profile than the average dog with a significant increase in calories. It's estimated that working dogs will consume 1.5 to 2.5 times more than the average pet in order to maintain a healthy weight. This is especially true for dogs working in extremely hot or cold climates as they may burn extra calories regulating their internal temperatures. The diet of a working dog also contains a higher protein and fat content, but caution should be taken as diets too high in fat may cause problems such as pancreatitis or digestive upset. Digestive upset may also occur if working dogs are fed immediately before or after strenuous physical activity. Many professional trainers recommend waiting at least an hour between food and exercise.

The exact ratio of carbohydrates, fats, and proteins needed by your working dog will vary according to his individual metabolism as well as the type of work he's doing. Dogs that are considered "sprint" athletes typically work in short, intense bursts. Most dog sports, such as agility and protection sports, will fall under this category. Canine athletes performing this type of work likely won't

Photo Courtesy of Therese Barrett

need a huge increase in calories and will do well on a food containing about 300 to 400 calories per cup. It's recommended that the dry matter content of carbs add up to approximately 40% to 50%. Dry matter fats should measure below about 15% and protein should be around 25%. Dry matter measuring is the most accurate method of measuring the contents of dog food as actual water content will vary by brand. The measurements are taken once all moisture has been removed. These numbers are typically available somewhere on the packaging of your dog's food, no matter what brand you use. The manufacturer may also have these numbers available on their website.

Dogs that work for longer periods of time, up to a few hours of intense physical activity, may need an increase of fat in their diet. A dry matter fat content of about 30% to 35% is recommended. Again, if your dog falls into this category, you'll need to adjust his daily calories as needed to maintain a healthy weight.

True endurance athletes are dogs that are engaged in physical activity for several hours or more at a time. These dogs will need the most nutrient-dense food, ideally around 500 to 600 calories per cup. They too will need an increase in fat and protein. Their food should measure around 30% to 35% of each, depending on the individual dog and the specific activities. These dogs will need a significantly higher number of calories each day when compared to less active dogs.

If you have any doubts about feeding your working dog, consider contacting a board-certified veterinary nutritionist. Many nutritionists specialize in working dog diets, so they'll be able to help you find the ideal diet for your Malinois. Though nutrition is just one aspect of caring for a working dog, it's not one that can be overlooked if you intend to keep him in top condition. Always seek the advice of professionals if you have any doubts or concerns.

Working dogs also require far more water than the average family canine companion. It's estimated that working dogs may consume 10 to 20 times more water. The amount of water needed to maintain hydration also increases as temperatures increase, so be sure that your working dog has access to clean fresh water when he needs it. While you should never limit your dog's water intake, it's important that you avoid letting him fill his stomach with water during or immediately after vigorous physical activity. Although Belgian Malinois are not particularly prone to bloat, a stomach full of water during an active training session could result in this life-threatening condition. Instead, you want to make sure your dog takes frequent drinks but in smaller amounts.

CHAPTER 15
Physical and Mental Exercise

The Importance of Physical Exercise

There are numerous benefits to providing your Belgian Malinois with adequate physical exercise. First, physical activity is crucial in maintaining a healthy weight. In addition to proper portion control, exercise can help keep your dog slim and fit. Without adequate physical activity, your Malinois is at risk of becoming overweight or obese, which can put excess strain on his joints and put him at risk of developing weigh-related health problems such as arthritis, diabetes, and heart disease.

Physical activity is also a great way to provide your Malinois with mental stimulation and prevent the development of boredom-related behavioral problems. The new sights and smells that your dog will experience with even a brisk walk around the neighborhood provide him with entertainment that just isn't possible

Photo Courtesy of Darcy Seeger

Photo Courtesy of Denise Casey

lying around on the sofa all day. Unless your dog is provided with these types of opportunities, it's likely that he'll seek entertainment around your house in the form of chewing, digging, or escaping. The more tired your Malinois is, the more likely he is to be well behaved.

However, there is no set amount of physical activity that you must give your dog each day. How much physical exercise your Belgian Malinois needs will depend on his age, energy level, and overall health. Typically, puppies and seniors will have less stamina than fit adult dogs. Any dog suffering from health problems is likely to need less exercise as well. Most healthy adult Belgian Malinois will do well with one to three hours of physical exercise each day.

Of course, this doesn't mean you need to walk your dog for three hours straight. This time can include walks, hikes, training sessions, or even vigorous play sessions. It can also be spread throughout the day, so if you only have time for a brisk walk around the neighborhood in the morning, you can make it up to your dog when you get home from work. Puppies and older dogs will typically prefer shorter, more frequent activities, while fit adults may do well with sessions requiring more physical endurance. If you do need to split your Malinois' activity up throughout the day, it's generally recommended to do as long of a session as possible in the morning so that your dog will be more willing to relax quietly while you're away at work.

You should also consider mixing up the activities to keep your Malinois active and interested. The more variety you provide your dog, the happier he'll be and the stronger your relationship will be. Malinois love their families, so the more you can do with your dog the better. If you enjoy trail running, mountain biking, or even paddle boarding, consider taking your Malinois with you. You might also want to consider signing up for training classes. Learning basic obedience will not only exercise your dog, but it will help him to be a better companion. Even if you've never considered competing in dog sports, signing up for an agility or rally class might be a fun opportunity to spend some quality time with your Malinois while keeping him physically fit.

Photo Courtesy of
Brian and Shelly Glenn

Exercising Puppies

"Your Malinois will need lots of outdoor exercise. As a puppy this should all be free playing, not dedicated jogging for miles. Scent games are great for mental stimulation, or teaching your puppy new tricks."

JANET WOLFF
Stahlrosenhof Intl K-9

Most experts recommend avoiding strenuous physical exercise until your dog is at least 18 months of age. This is because strenuous activity can be damaging to a puppy's developing body. Until a dog's growth plates are fully closed, there is an increased risk of joint damage. Of course, this doesn't mean you shouldn't exercise your Malinois puppy at all, but you should definitely be cautious about how long or strenuous his exercise sessions are.

Training sessions should also be kept short, not only for the health of your puppy's joints, but for the sake of his short attention span. Typically, sessions between five and fifteen minutes in length are more than enough to be effective. These sessions can also be repeated throughout the day, but it's important to quit before your puppy gets tired or loses focus. If you notice that your Malinois begins to get distracted around seven minutes into the session, try quitting at about five minutes so you won't need to end on an exhausted or frustrated note. The more strenuous your training sessions are, the shorter they should be to prevent your dog from becoming unwilling or uncooperative in the next session.

When exercising your Belgian Malinois puppy, it's crucial that you allow him to set his own limits. If his play sessions extend to 20 minutes or more, that's perfectly fine, but don't expect to take him on a ten-mile hike through the mountains. Most puppies are aware of how much they can handle and will make it clear when they've had enough.

Once your puppy has been fully vaccinated, you might also want to consider signing him up for a puppy class. Many puppy classes are intended to not only teach him the basics of obedience or agility, but also provide him with socialization and an opportunity to play with other

FUN FACT
Dogs – or SEALs?

Most of the dogs that work with the elite Navy SEALs are Belgian Malinois, including one named Cairo who helped SEAL Team 6 take down Osama bin Laden in 2011. SEAL dogs wear special body armor and night-vision goggles.

puppies. It's a great way to teach him how to behave as well as giving him the chance to wear himself out with other puppies.

The Importance of Mental Exercise

"Mental exercise can be dealt with through obedience training. Believe it or not, training your dog in obedience really makes them think things through... as your Malinois will want to get it right. You will not be able to live with a Malinois who gets little to no exercise. The dog was bred to herd/work/do something. Lying around the house will not work for this breed, and (if not given an outlet for their energy) they may become destructive...mainly out of boredom."

RAYMOND FARBER
Farbenholt Kennels

As an intelligent, high-drive breed, mental stimulation is a crucial aspect of caring for any Belgian Malinois. Unless you're willing to provide your Malinois with an adequate amount of mental stimulation, he's likely to seek that stimulation elsewhere, which can result in destructive behavior. Belgian Malinois can quickly destroy a variety of furniture and household items in mere minutes if given the chance. Mental stimulation may not be able to guarantee the safety of the items in your home, but it makes it much less likely that your Malinois will take out his frustration on your furniture.

Though mental exercise is important to all Malinois, it's especially important for dogs with health or mobility problems. For puppies and senior dogs, an increase in mental stimulation may be able to make up for their lack of strenuous physical activity. Activities such as games, toys, and training sessions are ideal for engaging your dog's mind without overstressing his body. Anything involving interesting scents is especially interesting to most dogs.

Remember, activities engaging your dog's mind are likely to be far more exhausting than those that only engage his body. It's possible that your Malinois will be able to hike all day and still want to play a vigorous game of fetch when he gets home but gets tired after just 15 minutes or so of strenuous mental exertion. This is completely normal for any dog, so it's important that you keep your training sessions short and relatively simple. Try focusing on just one or two tasks per session if possible. If your Malinois gets confused by what you're asking of him, go back to something simple that he knows and end the session there. If you keep pushing him beyond what his mental endurance can handle, you risk frustration and he may be less willing to do what you ask in future training sessions.

Photo Courtesy of
Aaron Zenz

Playtime

"Belgian Malinois require daily exercise, running around the yard or playing fetch for a few minutes is not enough. Hiking, walking, running are all great exercise that bond the owner and dog. Obedience, agility, herding, scentwork, or trick training are all great mental exercise for your Malinois."

SUZANNE J BELGER
Desert Mountain Malinois

*Photo Courtesy of
Marsha Esslinger*

Photo Courtesy of
Sara Golac

Play is an essential part of your dog's physical and mental exercise routine. Not only does it work his body and mind together but playing is a great stress reliever to help him unwind from stressful training sessions. Some Malinois may prefer to play alone with toys, while others prefer a playdate with a canine buddy. If your dog prefers to enjoy a good chew toy on his own, you can also try hiding food or treats to keep him mentally and physically engaged as he attempts to figure out how to remove the food. To increase the challenge, you may also consider freezing the treats inside the toy. Puzzle toys are also a great way to provide your dog with a mental challenge. They're typically made of either wood or plastic and feature lots of flaps, sliding doors, and cups that must be maneuvered in order to access the tasty treats contained inside. Puzzle toys also come in varying levels of difficulty, so you can rotate them to provide your dog with a new challenge every time you give him a treat-filled toy.

Some Belgian Malinois prefer the companionship of another dog rather than a solo play session. If you don't have another dog at home, consider setting up regular playdates with dogs belonging to friends and family members. Regular play sessions with other dogs are a great way to keep your Malinois physically and mentally stimulated and are also an excellent way to socialize him with other friendly and playful dogs. The more opportunities you can give your dog to play with his furry best friends, the happier and calmer he's likely to be. However, it's important to be certain that any future playmates are friendly so that you don't get your dog into a situation that makes him uncomfortable or could set back his socialization. Only allow your dog to play with other dogs that you know and trust to prevent any fights or injuries. For this reason, it's also important that all

Photo Courtesy of
Shayne Piront

play with dogs outside your home be supervised so that you can intervene if things go south.

If your Belgian Malinois would rather play with his beloved humans, you may also consider taking a more hands-on approach to his play sessions. A game of chase, tug, or fetch will exercise you both and strengthen your bond. Another fun activity to do together is to hide treats around your home or yard and allow your Malinois to search for them using his sense of smell. This scavenger hunt style game is perfect for mentally stimulating all dogs but is especially useful for puppies and seniors who may not have the physical ability for more vigorous types of play.

Every Belgian Malinois is an individual, so your dog's favorite type of play may differ from other Malinois. Don't be afraid to experiment with different games or types of play to find out what he likes best. If your Malinois seems disinterested in that new squeaky toy you bought him, don't despair, he just may prefer a good game of fetch or tug rather than playing with it on his own. No matter how your Malinois likes to play, it's important that you provide him with as many opportunities to play as possible to keep him happy and healthy.

CHAPTER 16
Grooming

Coat Basics

The coat of the Belgian Malinois is relatively low maintenance. The short, double coat requires occasional brushing and bathing only when necessary. Double coats consist of a stiffer, weatherproof outer coat and a soft dense undercoat. Combined, the two layers of coat protect the Malinois from both the heat and the cold. Like most double-coated breeds, the Belgian Malinois should never be shaved. To do so would be to remove the dog's protection from extreme temperatures. Additionally, many double-coated dogs who have been shaved down have trouble growing their coat back afterwards or experience a change in coat texture.

Belgian Malinois are not considered heavy shedders. Most shed lightly throughout the year but will blow their coat twice per year. Most Malinois owners are comfortable brushing their dogs a few times per week. During periods of seasonal heavy shedding, daily brushing is recommended to remove the loose hair and prevent it from being spread throughout your home. Typically, bathing should be done every 8 to 12 weeks to remove excess dirt and oil from the coat.

Essential Grooming Tools

Even if you plan on sending your Malinois to a professional groomer, you'll still need to invest in a few essential grooming tools to keep your Belgian Malinois looking and feeling his best. To cut back on the amount of hair found throughout your home, you should purchase a quality brush to use on his coat a few times per week. The type of brush you use on your Malinois will depend on your own preferences, but there are a few options that work best with double coats. A rubber curry brush can be used wet or dry to help remove dead hair and stimulate blood flow to the skin. Many dogs enjoy being brushed with rubber curry brushes as they find the massaging sensation to be relaxing. Wire slicker brushes can also be used, but they may not remove the dead hair as quickly as other types of brushes. Deshedding brushes are ideal for use during heavy seasonal shedding, but they must be used carefully to avoid damage to the hair or skin. If you're unsure of which type of brush suits you and your dog best, consider trying a few different options or asking your local groomer for advice.

If you plan on grooming your Belgian Malinois yourself, you'll want to buy a high-quality dog shampoo. The specific type of shampoo you choose will depend on your dog's needs as well as your own preferences. If your dog suffers from any skin or coat issues, a soothing oatmeal or medicated shampoo may be best. If he's in good health, you might choose the shampoo according to your favorite scent. Shampoos formulated to help with deshedding are also available for use during shedding season. Try to find a shampoo with ingredients you can actually pronounce. The more natural the ingredients are, the less likely your dog is to develop skin irritation. It's important to note that many natural shampoos are made with low sudsing ingredients, so you'll see fewer bubbles than with shampoos with more artificial ingredients. This doesn't mean your dog won't be clean when you're done, it just means you'll spend less time rinsing bubbles out of your dog's coat.

Some Malinois owners choose to follow their favorite shampoo with a coat conditioner, but this is an optional step. Dogs with healthy coats will be fine without a conditioner, but if your dog is shedding heavily or suffering from skin or coat problems, consider using a conditioner formulated to help with the specific problem. Conditioners can cause the coat to take longer to dry, so if it's chilly out you might consider skipping the conditioner until the weather warms up. If you feel that your Malinois' coat could use additional nourishment but don't want the added step of using conditioner in the bath, you might also consider using a leave-in spray conditioner afterwards.

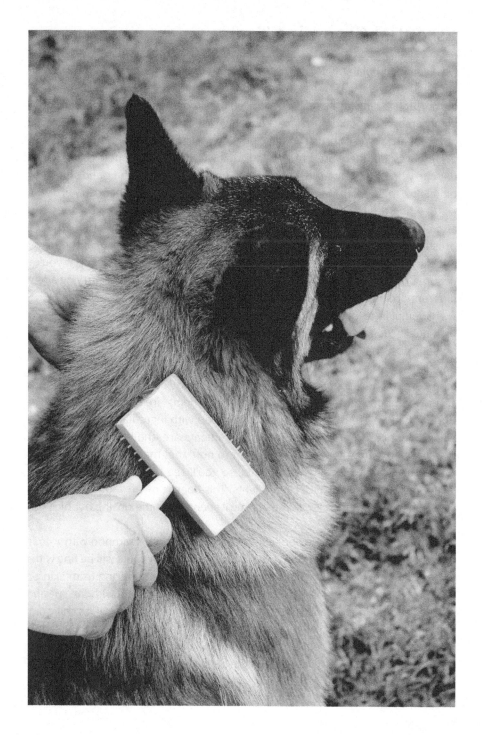

If you decide to trim your Belgian Malinois' nails yourself, you'll need to decide whether you want to buy a nail trimmer or grinder. If you decide on a trimmer, you'll find that the majority of professional groomers will recommend scissor-style clippers over guillotine-style. This is because scissor-style trimmers tend to make cleaner cuts and reduce the risk of crushing damage to the nails. Many professional groomers will also recommend nail grinders. Grinders are available in either corded or cordless models and can help reduce your chances of cutting your dog's nails too short. Your choice of nail trimming method will depend on your and your dog's preferences, so choose the tool that works best for your situation.

Bathing

"I would suggest baths about every 5 months (depending on how dirty the dog gets in its daily life). And I would suggest that baths start early - maybe even at 5 months and even if the dog doesn't need one. Getting different hands on the dog will help the dog accept strangers handling/touching them. This will also help when the dog has to go to a veterinarian."

RAYMOND FARBER
Farbenholt Kennels

Fortunately, the Belgian Malinois has a relatively low maintenance coat, so you won't need to spend a lot of your spare time bathing your new companion. Most groomers recommend bathing your dog every 8 to 12 weeks, depending on your dog's lifestyle and the condition of his skin and coat. While it can be tempting to bathe your dog often to keep him smelling fresh despite his daily outdoor romps, bathing too frequently can have a detrimental effect on your dog's coat. It can dry out both the skin and coat, resulting in irritation and dandruff. However, bathing should not be done too infrequently either. Otherwise, your dog's coat can build up too much dirt, oil, and dead hair, which can also cause a variety of skin problems.

When bathing your Belgian Malinois, take care to get the shampoo down to the skin so you're not just washing the top layer of the coat. Consider using a rubber curry brush in the bath to evenly distribute the shampoo if you're having trouble getting through the coat with just your hands. Professional bathing systems, such as the Hydrosurge, can help, but they can be quite expensive for the average dog owner.

It's crucial that you use caution when scrubbing around your dog's more sensitive areas. If you're using a rubber curry comb to help distribute the shampoo through his coat, avoid using it on his face and the bony parts of his legs. These areas are more delicate and should be washed by hand to avoid injury. Additionally, you should be careful to avoid getting shampoo in your Malinois' ears and eyes. It can be helpful to put cotton balls in your dog's ears to prevent the water from running down into them, but you must remember to take the cotton balls out afterwards. You may also want to consider having eye rinse on hand, just in case you get shampoo in your dog's eyes. However, if you use caution while washing these areas, you shouldn't have any problems.

Although shampooing your dog's coat thoroughly is important, it's even more crucial that you completely rinse the shampoo from his coat afterwards. Shampoo residue in the coat can cause skin irritation and hot spots, so you must be sure that you have rinsed the coat as thoroughly as possible. Once you believe you've removed all shampoo residue, rinse once more just to be sure. If you choose to follow with a conditioner, you'll need to be sure to rinse the conditioner from his coat just as you did the shampoo.

If you take your Belgian Malinois to a professional groomer, it's likely that the groomer will dry him with a high-velocity dryer. High-velocity dryers, or force dryers, are powerful enough to separate the coat and dry it down to the skin. The dryers are also capable of blowing out dead skin and hair, saving you brushing

*Photo Courtesy of
Briana Haydel*

time later. For the home groomer, high-velocity dryers can save a lot of time, but they can be expensive and tricky to handle if you're unfamiliar with their usage. If you'd like to use a high-velocity dryer on your Malinois at home, consider asking your local groomer for advice. He or she may also be able to help teach your dog to stand politely during the process.

If you'd prefer to do more than towel dry your dog, you might also consider using a handheld dryer. If the dryer of your choice produces heat, you should also be careful of how close you place the dryer to the dog's skin to avoid burning him. It can be helpful to have one hand on the dryer and one hand on the dog at all times, both for the safety of the dog as well as keeping the dryer at a safe distance. Of course, towel drying is always the easiest method of drying your Malinois' coat but be aware that he may shake excess water and hair all over your home and furniture before he is fully dry.

Brushing

Most owners and groomers recommend brushing Belgian Malinois between one and three times per week for the majority of the year. This should be enough to minimize the hair found around your home between trips to the groomer. During the Malinois' twice yearly blowout, you may need to brush your dog every day. It's important that you begin brushing your new dog as soon as possible after bringing him home so that he gets used to the process. It will be a lifelong experience for him, so the sooner he accepts it the better.

Whether you choose to use a rubber curry brush or a deshedding brush, it's important that you brush with enough pressure to remove the dead hair, but not so much that you scratch the skin or cause discomfort. If you're unfamiliar with the correct usage of the brush of your choice, or need help choosing the right tools, consult your local groomer for professional advice.

HELPFUL TIP
Brush Weekly

While you don't need to worry about a Mal's fur getting tangled, they do shed quite a bit more than you might expect. Brush your Malinois at least once a week with a rubber curry-style brush, slicker brush, and a greyhound comb to help reduce shedding. Be careful with de-shedding tools—you can damage your dog's skin or coat if you're too enthusiastic with them!

Cleaning Eyes and Ears

Due to their upright ears, Belgian Malinois are not particularly prone to developing ear infections, but they can happen when basic ear care is neglected. Typically, this occurs after moisture enters the ear canal while swimming or bathing. When combined with your dog's natural body heat, the moisture creates the perfect environment for yeast and bacteria to thrive. It's important to clean your Malinois' ears regularly, usually after swimming or bathing.

Symptoms of ear infections can include scratching at one or both ears, redness, swelling, or an unpleasant odor coming from his ears. Unfortunately, there is no effective at-home remedy for ear infections and you'll need to take your Malinois to the vet for a proper diagnosis. As infections can be caused by either bacteria or yeast, your vet will need to swab the affected ear to determine the correct course of treatment. Unless neglected for long periods of time, ear infections are easy to treat with either oral or topical medications.

When cleaning your Malinois' ears at home, you'll need to purchase an ear cleaner and cotton balls. Ear cleaners may or may not have alcohol in them and it's important to recognize the difference between them. Cleaners containing alcohol are ideal for post-swim ear cleaning as the alcohol will help dry the ear. However, if your dog has an infection already or just has particularly sensitive ears, the alcohol can cause a painful burning sensation. If that is the case, non-alcohol-based cleaners are recommended.

Cleaning your Belgian Malinois' ears is a relatively simple process. First, wet a cotton ball with the ear cleaner and squeeze out the excess liquid before inserting the cotton ball into your dog's ears. Gently wipe around the ear canal. Don't be afraid to gently clean as deep into the ear as your finger can reach. Your finger is too big to be able to reach the more sensitive structures of the ear. However, it's important that you use only your fingers and a cotton ball and never a cotton swab. Cotton swabs are narrow enough that they are capable of reaching delicate structures within the ear and you can seriously damage your dog's ear. Once you believe that you've cleaned away all of the visible dirt and ear wax, you can go over the ear once more with a dry cotton ball to absorb the remaining cleaner. This step isn't necessary with most cleaners, but it can help prevent your dog from wiping it all over your furniture or carpet.

Few Belgian Malinois develop tear stains, so cleaning your dog's eyes will likely not be an issue. If your dog does start producing excess tears, you may want to take him to the vet prior to any at-home treatments to rule out any serious issues. It's normal for many dogs to develop a bit of crusty discharge at the corners of their eyes, so you may need to wipe that away on occasion. Eye cleaners are available in either a liquid form or pre-soaked pads. If you choose the liquid form, you can apply it to a cotton ball or pad, or even a soft cloth, in order to gently wipe away any discharge around your Malinois' eyes. Most of these cleaners are safe for use around eyes, but you should use caution so as not to poke or scratch your dog's eyes with the cloth or your fingers.

Trimming Nails

"Belgian Malinois should have their nails done weekly to avoid over-grown nails and ugly feet. Long nails may cause splayed feet and that will affect the dog's ability to work and have fun."

SUSIE WILLIAMSON
Merson Belgian Malinois

Trimming your Belgian Malinois' nails should be a regular part of his grooming routine, whether you do it yourself or have a professional take care of it. Unfortunately, there is no set schedule for nail trims as it depends on how fast your individual dog's nails grow. Some grow faster than others and if your dog walks frequently on pavement, rather than soft dirt or grass, you may find that nail trims need to be done less frequently. Some owners may find that weekly nail trims are ideal for keeping their dog's nails short and tidy, while others would prefer to do it monthly. In the beginning, it can be helpful to do nail trims more frequently so your Malinois gets used to the process.

Before you trim your Malinois' nails, you'll need to locate the nail's blood supply, known as the quick. You'll want to avoid the quick, as cutting it can be painful for your dog and it can bleed quite profusely. If your Malinois has a few light-colored nails, it will be relatively easy, but it can be difficult to see on dark-colored nails. You'll need to trim the nail in thin layers to avoid cutting too far. Keep an eye out for a darker-colored circle in the middle of the nail. If it has been some time since your Malinois has had his nails trimmed, it may take several layers before you see it, but once you see the dark area in the center of the nail, you need to stop trimming. This is the end of the quick and if you continue to trim, you'll end up hurting your dog. As you repeat this process for each of your dog's nails, don't forget to trim his dewclaws if he has any.

If you'd rather not trim your Belgian Malinois' nails yourself, your groomer or vet would be happy to do so. Nail trims are typically quite inexpensive, less than $20 in most areas. Many places also offer the option of either clipping or grinding, so if you or your dog has preference, they can use the method of your choice. Professionals are also more capable of handling difficult or nervous dogs, so they'll be able to do it more efficiently and quickly than the average owner anyway. If you're interested in learning how to trim your dog's nails, they may also be able to show you the correct way of handling and trimming.

Brushing Your Dog's Teeth

If you're interested in maintaining your Belgian Malinois' dental health at home, it's crucial that you understand that you must brush your dog's teeth every day in order for it to have any real effect. Think about how healthy your teeth would be if you only brushed them on occasion, rather than every day. Tartar tends to build up quickly, depending on your dog's diet, and can quickly cause problems if not dealt with. Periodontal disease can be painful and can cause your dog to have difficulty eating and he may even lose teeth if it's left untreated. Bacteria from the plaque and tartar on your dog's teeth can also enter your dog's bloodstream, causing infection in vital organs. Fortunately, dental disease is a preventable condition with at-home care and regular veterinary checkups.

On your next trip to your favorite pet store, check out their selection of toothbrushes and toothpaste. Many dog toothbrushes look similar to the ones you use on your own teeth, but you may also be able to find ones that fit over your finger or brush all surfaces of the tooth at once. The type you use will depend on your own preferences, so if you don't trust that your dog won't bite down on the toothbrush,

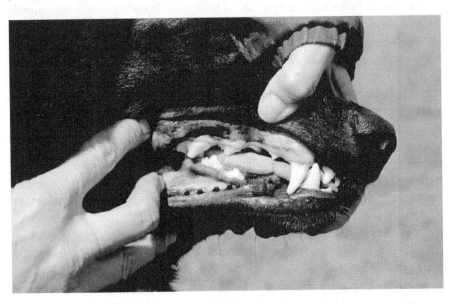

don't use the type that you wear on your finger. Some owners even buy toothbrushes designed for human children as they are the right size and softness. However, it's important that you only use toothpaste designed for dogs. Human toothpaste often contains ingredients that can be toxic to dogs if ingested. Doggy toothpaste comes in a variety of flavors including vanilla, chicken, beef, and more. You can also make your own toothpaste out of baking soda and water if you'd prefer a more natural approach.

To brush your Malinois' teeth, you'll need to place a small amount of toothpaste on the toothbrush of your choice. Gently lift your dog's lips out of the way and softly scrub the surface of each tooth, just as you would when brushing your own teeth. Do not brush vigorously as you may cause discomfort and your dog may pull away. If he seems uncertain about the process, be sure to let him sniff and lick the toothbrush and toothpaste a bit before starting to brush. As always, encourage his patience with plenty of verbal praise during the process and affection afterwards.

Even if you do choose to brush your Belgian Malinois' teeth each and every day, he's still going to need regular dental checkups with his veterinarian. Most vets recommend dental cleanings every six to twelve months. Healthy adults may need to be seen less often, but senior dogs often require more frequent visits. Ask your veterinarian about how often he or she would like to see your dog for checkups. Dental cleanings are a relatively simple and incredibly safe procedure that requires your dog to undergo anesthesia for a brief time. If you have any questions or concerns about the procedure or what you can do to better maintain your Malinois' dental health, ask your veterinarian at your next appointment.

When Professional Help Is Necessary

There is no right time to seek professional help. Whether you're struggling with grooming your Belgian Malinois yourself or would simply prefer to have someone else handle it, don't be afraid to contact your local groomer. Groomers are experts in handling difficult or nervous dogs and know how to gain a dog's trust. They are capable of taking a wild, unruly dog and teaching him to stand patiently for grooming in just a few sessions in most cases. In fact, once your Malinois gets to know his groomer, he may begin to get excited whenever you take him. Paying a professional groomer to maintain your Malinois' coat and nails is often the best choice for owners that are unwilling or unable to groom their dog themselves. Just remember to budget accordingly for grooming services and be sure to tip your groomer generously, even if you're just taking your dog in for regular nail trims.

CHAPTER 17
Basic Health Care

Visiting the Vet

I t's crucial that you take your Belgian Malinois in for regular checkups with your veterinarian throughout his lifetime. Most vets will recommend an exam every six to twelve months, depending on your dog's current health and age. While it may seem excessive to take your dog to the vet that often if nothing is obviously wrong with him, it's important that your vet is able to see your dog frequently enough to catch any problems before they have a serious effect on your dog's health. Many serious conditions can worsen quickly, so it's crucial that your vet has the opportunity to spot them early. Your Belgian Malinois will also need regular vaccinations, deworming, and dental checkups. Additionally, seeing your vet often will give you the chance to ask about any concerns you may have about your Malinois' health or weight.

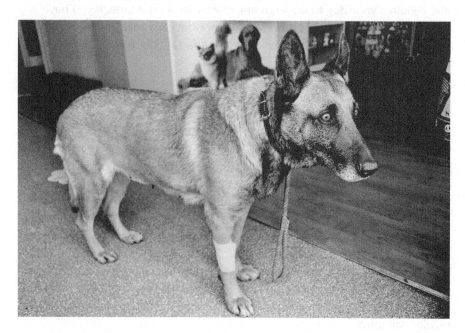

Allergies

One of the most common problems affecting dogs of all breeds and backgrounds is allergies. Allergies typically appear in dogs over six months of age, though most are not diagnosed until after one or two years of age. Though some allergies are believed to have a genetic component, most allergies are a result of a hypersensitivity of your dog's immune system. The most common allergens that cause these reactions are food, plants, insects, or other animals.

Symptoms of allergies can vary according to the cause of the allergic reaction. The most common symptoms are generalized or localized itching, sneezing, coughing, and discharge from the nose or eyes. It's common for dogs with food allergies to also experience vomiting or diarrhea. Food allergies typically show up as digestive upset and more generalized reactions, while reactions to external allergens such as insects will result in more localized itching or inflammation. Inhalant allergies, such as pollen, can also cause respiratory problems.

The specific treatment your veterinarian will prescribe will depend on the cause of your dog's allergic reaction. Diagnosing allergies can be somewhat difficult, so it's important to be patient while your veterinarian works to determine the cause of your dog's discomfort. If your Malinois is allergic to a certain protein in his diet, for example, you may need to perform an elimination diet to determine the specific allergen. If your dog has environmental allergies, it can be difficult to determine the allergen, but your vet may treat your dog with anti-inflammatory or antihistamine medication, usually either oral or injectable. Therapeutic shampoos or ointments may also be prescribed.

It's important to discuss any potential allergies with your vet as soon as possible because without treatment, severe skin irritation, hot spots, and hair loss may occur. Respiratory symptoms should be addressed immediately, so if your Malinois appears to be having trouble breathing due to an allergic reaction, you should take him to the vet right away.

FUN FACT
Skydiving Dogs

One reason that the Belgian Malinois is a more popular military dog breed than the German Shepherd is that they're lighter, which makes them easier to skydive with. Military parachutists will tandem skydive with their dog strapped to them. Some Malinois are even trained to jump on their own!

Fleas and Ticks

External parasites are common occurrences, but they can carry dangerous diseases, so it's important to seek treatment as soon as possible. Many external parasites can affect not only your Belgian Malinois, but your human family as well. Fleas frequently carry tapeworms and bartonellosis and can cause anemia. Many dogs also develop flea allergy dermatitis, which is when a dog's immune system reacts to the flea's saliva. Flea allergy dermatitis can cause symptoms such as skin inflammation, severe itching, and even hair loss. Ticks are also common carriers of diseases such as ehrlichiosis, Rocky Mountain spotted fever, Lyme disease, and babesiosis. Regular flea and tick prevention is a crucial part of keeping your entire family safe from disease.

The climate you live in will affect how frequently you need to administer flea and tick prevention. Warm climates with mild winters are more likely to have year-round flea and tick problems than those that have particularly cold seasons. In cold climates, it's possible your veterinarian may recommend only treating your Malinois during the summer months. No matter where you live, it's best to discuss flea and tick prevention with your veterinarian so you can get accurate advice based on your specific area. It's important to note that many boarding and doggy daycare facilities require dogs to be treated for fleas and ticks prior to staying with them, so if your dog is not current, he may need to be treated before he will be allowed to stay at the facility.

When deciding what flea and tick treatment is best for your Belgian Malinois, you should ask your veterinarian which product is right for your area and the species of parasites your dog may be exposed to. Most flea and tick prevention products are sold in plastic vials, which are broken and then applied to the back of your dog's neck. You'll need to part the hair to apply the product directly to the skin, as it will have little effect if it's applied to the top layer of hair. This process will likely need repeated every four to six weeks, depending on the specific product.

Most experts recommend avoiding flea and tick collars if possible. Though they may be convenient, they can cause problems, especially if you have other pets in your home. The insecticide tetrachlorvinphos is a common ingredient in flea and tick collars and can cause serious reactions. Cats in particular are incredibly sensitive to this chemical and reactions can be fatal. The most common reactions vary from hair loss and skin irritation to vomiting and diarrhea. Severe reactions may also cause seizures and death. The Environmental Protection Agency considers tetrachlorvinphos a carcinogen, so you would also potentially be exposing your human family members to a dangerous chemical if you choose to use these products.

*Photo Courtesy of
Elysia Bistrica*

Internal Parasites

The prevention of internal parasites should also be a regular part of your Belgian Malinois' veterinary care routine. Most internal parasites, such as worms, can cause serious health issues if left untreated, so it's crucial that you deworm your Malinois on a regular basis. Like external parasites, the specific internal parasites that your dog may pick up will depend on where you live. Similarly, many internal parasites can also be transferred from animals to humans, and children can be particularly susceptible to infection.

Intestinal worms are by far the most common internal parasites found in dogs in most area. Puppies are especially prone to internal parasites, which are most frequently acquired from adult dogs in the home. Worms are most often passed from one dog to another when one consumes the eggs or larvae located

Photo Courtesy of
Paul Johnson

in contaminated water, soil, food, or feces. The most common types of worms in dogs are hookworms, roundworms, tapeworms, and whipworms. Protozoa such as giardia and coccidia may also infect your Belgian Malinois' digestive tract.

Though the majority of internal parasites affect the digestive tract, heartworms are found in the heart and bloodstream. They are passed from animal to animal through mosquitos as they feed on the blood of infected and uninfected animals. Heartworm is more complicated to treat than other internal parasites and treatment can take months to finish. During this time, the affected dog's activity must be limited as the dying worms can block vital arteries. Severe infections can result in death if left untreated. However, like many other types of parasite, heartworm is easy to prevent by administering a chewable tablet each month.

Symptoms of internal parasites may include vomiting, diarrhea, weight loss, lethargy, and coughing. Puppies and dogs with an extremely heavy parasite load may appear malnourished, but with a distended belly. In these cases, anemia is also common. It is also possible that a dog may not exhibit any symptoms at all, so it's important to have your veterinarian check for parasites on a regular basis.

The detection of intestinal worms and protozoa is performed through a fecal exam, where your veterinarian will examine a small sample of your dog's feces under a microscope. The eggs or larvae will be visible, and the vet can determine what type of parasite is present so the correct treatment can be prescribed. To detect heartworm, a small sample of blood must be collected and mixed with a chemical solution before placing it into a disposable testing device. Results will be available after about fifteen minutes. Treatments for most species of parasites are relatively simple, usually either oral medication or injections. Depending on the type of parasite present, treatment can vary from just a couple of days to several months. However, regular deworming and frequent testing can help reduce the likelihood that your Malinois develops a parasitic infection serious enough to affect his health.

Vaccinations

Whether you've brought home a puppy or adult Belgian Malinois, vaccinations are sure to be a regular part of your new dog's life. Core vaccines, such as rabies, parvovirus, and distemper, will be administered throughout your dog's life. Non-core vaccines like Bordetella or leptospirosis may also need to be administered, depending on where you live and the lifestyle your dog leads.

Core vaccines typically come in a single syringe containing antibodies for a variety of diseases. The DHPP, or five-way vaccine, is the most common and protects against parvovirus, distemper, hepatitis, parainfluenza, and adenovirus cough. Puppies usually receive the DHPP vaccine at six, twelve, and sixteen weeks of age. As adults, dogs may receive the vaccine either yearly or every three years, depending on local laws and your veterinarian's recommendation.

Rabies is the only vaccine required by law in the United States and cannot be given prior to 16 weeks of age. The first time a dog receives the rabies vaccine, it's typically only good for a year, but it may be administered every three years thereafter depending on your vet's advice as well as local laws.

Non-core vaccines may also be recommended by your veterinarian and may include leptospirosis, rattlesnake venom, and Lyme disease. If you frequently board your Malinois or take him to doggy daycare or the groomer, he may also need to get the Bordetella vaccine, which vaccinates against kennel cough. Non-core vaccines do not last as long as core vaccines, so it's important to be aware that if you choose to give these to your Malinois, they may need to be administered much more frequently than core vaccines, sometimes as often as every six months.

Though most dogs receive vaccines with few to no problems, allergic reactions are always possible. For particularly sensitive dogs, it can help to only give one vaccine at a time, so if you believe your Malinois may react badly, you can discuss this option with your vet. Signs of an allergic reaction may include swelling of the face or paws, hives, lethargy, and vomiting. Swelling and pain around the injection site are also possible. More severe reactions may also include seizures and difficulty breathing, which will require immediate treatment. If you don't know how your dog will react to vaccines, it can be helpful to stay in the vicinity of the clinic for about twenty minutes to make sure you're close to help should he develop a reaction. Without immediate treatment, severe reactions can be life-threatening.

Depending on where you live, titer testing may also be a legal alternative to yearly core vaccines. A blood sample is taken and examined to measure the antibodies present. If the antibody levels are high enough, the dog can skip the vaccine until a later time, but if the levels are too low, he will need to be revaccinated. Titer testing is only available for core vaccines as non-core vaccines don't last long. As titer testing can be more expensive than regular vaccines, it would be difficult to justify the cost for titer testing for non-core vaccines in most cases. Titer testing can be a safer alternative to yearly vaccinations for dogs that experience vaccine reactions, though you must be willing to budget accordingly.

Holistic Alternatives

If you're interested in having your Belgian Malinois live a more natural life-style, you may want to consider finding a holistic veterinarian. If you think that holistic medicine is just herbs and acupuncture, you may be pleasantly surprised to learn that it is instead a combination of conventional and alternative therapies. Holistic veterinarians are required to attend the same veterinary schools as tra-ditional vets and will often treat pets with the same medications and procedures used by clinics across the country. It's likely that those conventional treatments may also be combined with alternative therapies like acupuncture, herbal sup-plements, and chiropractic adjustments.

Holistic veterinary care can be particularly beneficial to dogs suffering from chronic conditions or conditions that have been difficult to treat using more tradi-tional therapies. Holistic medicine differs from conventional medicine as it treats the body as a whole, rather than as individual parts. For example, if your Belgian Malinois is suffering from a skin condition, a holistic veterinarian may choose to use a combination of nutritional changes, herbal supplements, and topical med-ications. Rather than focus on just the skin, holistic vets would work to improve your dog's overall health in order to address the specific issue. Though conven-tional medicine should always be sought in an emergency, many owners find it helpful to seek a different solution to their dog's chronic health problems.

If you would like to find a holistic veterinarian in your area, the American Holistic Veterinary Medical Association has a list of vets in the United States and Canada available on their website. You'll be able to search through vets by the species they treat and the specific treatments they offer. This can be helpful in finding the right vet to address your Malinois' individual needs.

Pet Insurance

As the cost of veterinary care continues to rise, pet insurance is also rising in popularity among dog owners who seek a way to help cover the cost of their pet's healthcare. There are a variety of companies offering policies that differ in coverage and cost, so if you're interested in pet insurance you may need to shop around to find the right plan. It's important to be aware that just as with human health insurance, some dogs may cost more to cover or may be denied coverage due to age or preexisting conditions. Each company will have different require-ments, so it's important to do your research before purchasing a policy.

You should also be aware that unlike human health insurance, pet insurance usually doesn't cover the costs of preventative care. Those yearly exams and

Photo Courtesy of Holly Spencer

vaccinations will need to be paid for out of pocket, so you'll have to budget accordingly. There may be a few companies that offer coverage for routine care, but the policies can be quite expensive. However, should your dog develop a serious illness or have an accident, pet insurance would help cover the cost of treatment.

Most pet owners are somewhat divided on the topic of pet insurance. Some swear by it and would never own a pet without it, while others would prefer to save their money each month in preparation for potential emergencies. Those who have reaped the benefits of their plans are usually avid supporters, but owners of healthy adult dogs may pay premiums for years without actually needing coverage. Since those monthly premiums for unused insurance plans can add up quickly, many owners choose instead to set that money aside each month to use in the event of an emergency illness or injury. It's up to you to decide whether pet insurance is right for you, so be sure to do plenty of research prior to purchasing any insurance policy.

CHAPTER 18

Health Concerns in Belgian Malinois

Genetic Testing

Though Belgian Malinois are considered to be a healthy dog breed, genetic testing is an important part of maintaining the health of the breed as a whole. The chances of your Malinois inheriting a genetic disorder will depend on his bloodlines. Reputable breeders work hard to ensure that they are breeding dogs that are as healthy as possible. They will often spend thousands

Photo Courtesy of Diana Myers

Photo Courtesy of
Stuart McRae

of dollars to test for genetic disorders to ensure a dog is free from disease prior to entering the dog into their breeding program. Less reputable breeders, on the other hand, will be willing to overlook genetic testing in favor of selling dogs with specific coat colors or sizes to increase the price of their puppies.

Genetic testing can be performed by your veterinarian by collecting a sample of your dog's saliva. The sample is then submitted to a laboratory for genetic analysis. Once analyzed, the results can be evaluated by the breeder or submitted to the Canine Health Information Center to be made publicly available. By making the results publicly available, reputable breeders make it clear that they have nothing to hide. If you plan on breeding your Belgian Malinois, it's highly recommended to have him tested for genetic disorders prior to breeding. Otherwise, you aren't working to better the breed and eliminate the genetic disorders that affect Belgian Malinois.

FUN FACT
Celebrity Protector

After actress Eva Mendes got a restraining order against a stalker in 2011, she relied on her Belgian Malinois Hugo to protect her. Malinois make exceptional guard dogs thanks to their trainability and protective nature.

*Photo Courtesy of
Jordyn Verborg*

Hip and Elbow Dysplasia

Hip dysplasia is a painful condition that is common in large and medium-sized breeds of dog. The disease can be inherited but can also be caused by environmental factors such as injury or poor nutrition. Hip dysplasia occurs when the ball and socket of the hip joint do not fit together properly. The joint will rub or grind instead of sliding smoothly as it should. The grinding action will cause further deterioration and can potentially cause a full loss of function of the hip joint.

HELPFUL TIP
Pet Insurance

While the Belgian Malinois is a relatively healthy breed, any dog can get sick or injured, and those vet bills can add up quickly. You might want to consider getting pet insurance when you first bring your pup home. It doesn't cover preexisting conditions, and there's usually a waiting period before the coverage takes effect, so you don't want to wait until your Malinois gets sick or injured.

Symptoms include decreased range of motion of the hip joint, decreased activity, lameness, stiffness, and a reluctance to run and jump. Dogs with hip dysplasia may also display a unique hopping gate or atrophy in the thigh muscle. Dysplasia can be diagnosed through physical examination and X-rays. Treatments will vary depending on the severity, but may include nutritional changes, physical therapy, medication, or surgery.

Elbow dysplasia is similar to hip dysplasia in that it is a painful condition caused by a malformation of the elbow joint. However, many different conditions may be categorized as elbow dysplasia including fragmented coronoid process (FCP) and osteochondrosis (OCD), as well as cartilage anomaly. These different conditions simply specify the exact malformation of the elbow joint. As with hip dysplasia, elbow dysplasia will worsen over time and may result in total loss of joint function if left untreated. Symptoms include lameness and an unwillingness to stand up or walk. As elbow dysplasia may affect one or both joints, it can be difficult to detect when the lameness is symmetrical.

Eye Problems

Progressive Retinal Atrophy (PRA) is a genetic eye disease that can affect Belgian Malinois. It is a condition that specifically affects the photoreceptors of the eye. There are technically two different types of PRA. One is often referred to as retinal dysplasia and is usually diagnosed in puppies of about two or three

Photo Courtesy of
Kathleen Zafra

months of age. The second form of PRA is late onset and is not diagnosed until between three and nine years of age. In the early onset form, the condition is typically caused by the malformation of the photoreceptor cells and can lead to blindness at a young age. In the late onset form, the photoreceptor cells may develop normally, but will degenerate over time. One of the early symptoms of PRA is night blindness, so if your Malinois appears reluctant to walk around in the dark or bumps into things at night, it may be time to consult a veterinary ophthalmologist.

PRA is not a painful condition, but as a progressive disease, it will get worse over time and an affected dog's sight will deteriorate over time until the dog is completely blind. It typically takes about a year or two from onset to complete loss of vision, but it can happen more quickly. Unfortunately, there is no treatment or cure for PRA. Some vets may recommend antioxidant supplements to slow the deterioration of the photoreceptor cells, but there is no solid proof that these supplements will help. Most dogs can function well without eyesight as they tend to rely more on their other senses anyway. Dogs can quickly develop a mental map of familiar territory which will allow them to navigate without too much trouble. As PRA is a genetic condition, affected dogs should not be bred and all Malinois should be tested for PRA prior to being bred.

Preventing Illnesses

Properly managing your Belgian Malinois' lifestyle, healthcare, and nutrition can go a long way in preventing serious health problems. Though not every disease is preventable, as your dog's guardian, it's your responsibility to provide him with the best care you can afford. This includes feeding him a high-quality balanced diet and providing him with regular exercise, veterinary care, and grooming.

Regular veterinary appointments are one of the most important aspects of keeping your Belgian Malinois as healthy as possible. It may seem frivolous to take your perfectly healthy dog to the vet as often as every six months or so, but frequent examinations and testing are essential in making early treatment possible. Many health conditions progress quickly, so catching them in the early stages is crucial. Regular checkups also give you the opportunity to discuss less urgent concerns with your veterinarian such as your dog's weight, fitness, and behavior. Additionally, regular visits will keep your Belgian Malinois current on all vaccinations and parasite prevention treatments.

Photo Courtesy of
Cesilia Rodríguez

CHAPTER 19
The Aging Belgian Malinois

"The Malinois ages beautifully. While other breeds, I specifically have German Shepherd experience, go flat and can be ornery. The Malinois breed never loses that sense of "puppy". As long as their health permits they enjoy work, play, and exercise as they always have."

MARK ROTH JR.
BlackJack Malinois

Basics of Senior Dog Care

B elgian Malinois are typically considered to be geriatric, or senior, at around seven years of age. This doesn't mean that your dog will automatically begin displaying signs of old age on his seventh birthday, but instead you should begin to look for those signs as he nears this age. Depending on your Malinois, he may begin slowing down at an earlier age or he could continue acting like a healthy young dog well into his senior years. As Belgian Malinois typically have a lifespan of around 12 to 14 years, you can expect to begin seeing subtle changes in his body and behavior somewhere around seven years of age.

These changes can happen so slowly that you may not even recognize them at first. Perhaps your Malinois is sleeping more or just getting tired more quickly on hikes or during training sessions. Some older dogs can have difficulty getting out of bed in the morning due to muscle and joint stiffness. Deteriorating hearing and sight are also common in senior dogs, so it's important that you try not to startle your aging Malinois, especially if he's sleeping. Some older dogs may gain a significant amount of weight as their metabolism slows, but it's also possible for senior dogs to become quite thin. Many geriatric dogs will also require more frequent bathroom breaks as their bladders aren't as strong as they used to be. It's also possible for older dogs to suffer from cognitive dysfunction, or dementia, so you may notice behavioral changes or occasional confusion. As you notice these changes in your Belgian Malinois, it's important to adjust his care to accommodate his aging mind and body.

Photo Courtesy of
Vicky Traxell

Regular Vet Visits

"Listen to your dog and their body. If they start to get stiff, put them on a joint supplement, if they start to shed more, a fish oil supplement for coat and more brushing. Watch the teeth as they may need a dental cleaning as they get older. Slow down their exercise regimen if they start to slow down. Just watch your dog and love them!"

BETH ROOD
Roodhaus Belgian Malinois

Even if your senior Belgian Malinois seems healthy, most vets recommend more frequent checkups as your dog progresses through his golden years. If you were taking him to the vet for checkups once a year as a healthy adult, you should consider taking him every six months or so instead. This will give your vet the opportunity to catch any developing conditions early and will also give you the chance to discuss the changes associated with age with your vet. Many older dogs also require more frequent dental care, so professional dental cleanings may need to be scheduled more often.

It can be helpful to ask your veterinarian at each visit for recommendations to make your Malinois' transition into old age as easy as possible. Your vet may suggest changes in exercise or nutrition, or there may be medications available to help ease the pain of arthritis. It's likely that your vet may also simply recommend you bring your aging Malinois in for more frequent checkups.

Nutritional Changes

As your Belgian Malinois ages, his metabolism will slow, and you may need to adjust the number of calories he consumes each day. Whereas an active adult Malinois may consume a relatively high number of calories, an aging senior dog will often require an adjustment to maintain a healthy weight. If you continue to feed him a high number of calories, your dog may gain weight, which can put excess strain on his arthritic joints. This in turn may lead to less mobility and even more weight gain. In order to prevent the discomfort and health problems associated with obesity, it's crucial that you adjust your Malinois' portion sizes to accommodate the changes in his body and metabolism. You may also want to consider switching him to a food specifically formulated for senior dogs. These foods typically contain fewer calories, but also frequently contain other beneficial ingredients like glucosamine, chondroitin, and an increase in fiber content.

Though weight gain is common in older dogs, some aging Belgian Malinois may also find it difficult to keep weight on due to health problems or changes in appetite. Though they may have once found a variety of foods appetizing, some senior dogs will begin to turn their noses up at their favorite foods. For these types of dogs, it's important to find a food that appeals to them, which may mean changing a dog's diet entirely or just adding delicious toppers to his meals each day. If your Malinois has previously been fed kibble, you may consider switching to or adding in canned food. You may also want to try supplementing your aging dog's diet with raw or cooked food. As always, if you have any concerns about your senior dog's diet, it's best to consult a veterinary nutritionist for advice.

Photo Courtesy of Laura Moehring

You may also need to adjust your Belgian Malinois diet to accommodate any health conditions he may have developed as he has aged. Dogs with heart or kidney problems, for instance, may require a prescription diet rather than a food formulated for senior dogs. Arthritis can also be helped with nutritional supplements such as glucosamine, MSM, and chondroitin. Digestive issues are also common in old age, so you may want to ask your veterinarian about adding supplements such as probiotics, digestive enzymes, or fiber to your senior dog's diet. If you notice sudden changes in your dog's weight, or if he seems to be experiencing digestive upset more frequently, it's important to discuss this with your veterinarian as soon as possible. You'll need to rule out any health problems prior to changing or adjusting your Malinois' diet.

Exercising Your Senior Dog

"There should be far less jumping for older dogs, and (if possible) more swimming, so that there is less joint trauma. Owners should know their dog - and know when it's had enough exercise for the day. I normally give my older Malinois an aspirin (specific for dogs); if I see that they are uncomfortable/sore from the day's activities. This eases their pain associated with inflammation. Make your Malinois golden years golden! This is one very special breed."

RAYMOND FARBER
Farbenholt Kennels

A slowing metabolism combined with the ache of arthritic joints means that your Belgian Malinois will likely begin to slow down as he reaches his senior years. If he has certain health problems on top of the usual symptoms of old age, he may begin to find strenuous exercise uncomfortable. If this is the case, he may prefer lying around on the sofa all day instead of going for his usual weekend hike. However, it's important that you do not eliminate all physical activity from your senior Malinois' daily schedule. Exercise is essential to every dog's health, no matter their age, but you may need to make adjustments. Shorter, more frequent walks may be appropriate, or you might consider low-impact exercise such as swimming.

You should also consider adding more mental stimulation in place of strenuous physical activity. Mental stimulation is ideal for senior dogs to keep them active and busy without straining their bodies. It's not uncommon for a senior dog's body to age more quickly than their mind, so your dog may enjoy engaging in more mental challenges like puzzle toys or scent work.

You may also need to adjust your senior Belgian Malinois' environment in order to provide him with a safe place to exercise. Slick floors, flights of stairs, and hard surfaces like pavement can cause discomfort and injury in older dogs. Instead, consider playing a casual game of fetch on soft grass or take your dog for more frequent swims at the local pond. Not only will the softer surface reduce the discomfort on your dog's aging joints, but the change in scenery will help keep his mind sharp and engaged.

"If your aging Malinois wants to continue to do activities, let them. The activities may be more limited in nature, but it is better to allow them to continue to have some sort of activity. The majority of our dogs are still working the streets past 10 years old."

JANET WOLFF
Stahlrosenhof Intl K-9

Environmental Changes

While changing the environment where you exercise your aging Belgian Malinois is important, you may also need to make adjustments in your home in order to provide your senior dog with a safe and comfortable space. Since many geriatric dogs do not have the muscle strength they once had, you may notice your dog struggling to climb stairs or stay balanced on slick surfaces such as hardwood or linoleum. You should consider placing more rugs throughout your home or having your dog wear comfortable non-slip booties to give him a better grip. Special harnesses are also available to allow you to give your dog the assistance he needs to get upstairs if necessary.

FUN FACT
Healthy Dogs, Long Lives

Since it's such a common dog for military and police work (alongside other jobs), only the healthiest Mals get bred, resulting in one of the healthiest dog breeds around, especially for a large dog breed. They have few genetic health conditions, and the AKC lists their life expectancy at a whopping 14 to 16 years!

Cognitive changes can also cause older dogs to become confused more often, so you'll need to make sure that your dog can't get into trouble should he forget where he is. Whether he ends up in a stairwell, pool, or somewhere outdoors, it's important that you either keep an eye on your aging dog or limit his access to certain areas of your home in order to keep him safe. If your aging Malinois seems to struggle to climb up onto the sofa or bed, you might consider providing him with stairs or a lower comfortable alternative. Though many of these changes may not complement your décor, the wellbeing of your senior dog should always be your priority.

Preparing to Say Goodbye

As your Belgian Malinois ages and his health declines, it's important to begin planning for the end of your beloved family member's life. Though it can be difficult to know when it's time to say goodbye, it can happen quickly, so it's important to be prepared. Your Malinois' quality of life should always be the main factor in determining whether euthanasia is the best option. If your dog no longer seems to enjoy the things he once did, or his moments of suffering outnumber his moments of comfort, it may be time to make the decision to say goodbye. As this time approaches, it's important that you reflect on your much-loved companion's

Photo Courtesy of Erika Martinez

life and remember all of the happiness you have enjoyed together over the years. Saying goodbye is difficult, but remembering the joy your Malinois has brought to your family can help you navigate through the grieving process.

While some dogs pass peacefully in their sleep, others may need assistance in passing over the rainbow bridge in the form of humane assistance. Euthanasia is a painless procedure administered by a veterinarian. The veterinarian administers an overdose of an anesthetic drug called sodium pentobarbital. Once injected into the bloodstream, the drug causes the animal to peacefully fall asleep before gently stopping the heart. A veterinary technician usually holds the dog while he is lying down so that the drug can be safely injected into a vein, usually a front leg, via an intravenous catheter. If the dog is particularly confused, afraid, or in pain, a sedative may be used first to put the dog at ease. After the sodium pentobarbital is injected, unconsciousness occurs in mere seconds and the heart typically stops in less than a minute. The administering veterinarian will then confirm that the heart has stopped with the use of a stethoscope.

Your Belgian Malinois' final arrangements can be a difficult thing to discuss in the moment, but it can be helpful to make these arrangements in advance so that you can focus on your last moments together when the time comes. Many vets offer both in-home and in-office euthanasia services, so you can decide where you'd prefer to say goodbye. For some owners and dogs, saying goodbye in a sterile exam room can be stressful, while others may prefer not to have the memories of these final moments take place in their home. Whichever option you prefer, your veterinarian and his or her team are sure to be comforting and supportive though this difficult process. They have been through this many times and will be helpful in answering any questions you may have. The most important aspect of these final moments is that you are together with your Malinois. He will find comfort in knowing that his last moments will be with the person or people he has loved most throughout his life.

After saying goodbye, your veterinarian will probably have different options available for your Belgian Malinois' remains. If you would rather not deal with the remains yourself, your veterinary team will be happy to make appropriate arrangements. Many clinics also offer cremation services, where you may choose whether or not you'd like the ashes returned to you. If you know the time to say goodbye is approaching, you may want to discuss your options in advance so that you don't have to make any last-minute decisions during this stressful and emotional time.

Grief and Healing

The first few days and weeks after saying goodbye to your beloved Belgian Malinois will be especially difficult, but it will get easier with time. You should find comfort that you are not alone, as everyone who has been blessed with sharing their lives with these animals has gone through the same experience. Many owners choose to create a memorial for their dogs to help them remember their most cherished moments together. You can find personalized jewelry, garden stones, and tiles to memorialize your treasured companion. You might also consider channeling your grief into helping others by planting trees or gardens, volunteering at a local animal shelter, or making a monetary donation to a worthy cause. Helping animals or people in need can help some people navigate through their grief.

If you find yourself struggling to move on with the healing process, you might consider seeking the advice of a grief counselor or mental health professional. Everyone processes grief differently, so it's important that you find the right coping method to help you and your family through this difficult time. However you choose to heal, be sure to cherish the memories you have of your beloved Belgian Malinois and never forget the unconditional love you received.

Made in the USA
Monee, IL
29 July 2024

62883143R00109